KU-268-745

JOHN WYCLIFFE

Herald of the Reformation

Ellen Caughey

BARBOUR
PUBLISHING, INC.
Uhrichsville, Ohio

Other books in the "Heroes of the Faith" series:

Brother Andrew
Gladys Aylward
Dietrich Bonhoeffer
William and Catherine Booth
John Bunyan
William Carey
Amy Carmichael
George Washington Carver
Fanny Crosby
Frederick Douglass
Jonathan Edwards
Jim Elliot
Charles Finney
Billy Graham
C. S. Lewis
Eric Liddell
David Livingstone
Martin Luther
D. L. Moody
Samuel Morris

George Müller
Watchman Nee
John Newton
Florence Nightingale
Luis Palau
Francis and Edith Schaeffer
Charles Sheldon
Mary Slessor
Charles Spurgeon
John and Betty Stam
Billy Sunday
Hudson Taylor
William Tyndale
Corrie ten Boom
Mother Teresa
Sojourner Truth
John Wesley
George Whitefield

© 2001 by Barbour Publishing, Inc.

ISBN 1-58660-297-7

All rights reserved. No part of this publication may be reproduced or
transmitted in any form or by any means without written permission
of the publisher.

Published by Barbour Publishing, Inc., P.O. Box 719, Uhrichsville, OH 44683
http://www.barbourbooks.com

Cover illustration © Dick Bobnick.

Member of the
Evangelical Christian
Publishers Association

Printed in the United States of America.

JOHN WYCLIFFE

In memory of Wilse,
one of the lights of my life.

The Gospel telleth us the duty which falls to all the disciples of Christ, and also telleth us how priests, both high and low, should occupy themselves in the church of God and in serving Him. And first, Jesus Himself did do the lessons which He taught. The Gospel relates how Jesus went about in the places of the country, both great and small, as in cities and castles, or small towns; and this is to teach us to be useful generally to men, and not to be unwilling to preach to a people because they are few, and our name may not, in consequence, be great. For we should labour for God, and from Him hope for our reward. There is no doubt that Christ went into small uplandish towns, as to Bethphage, and Cana in Galilee; for Christ went to all those places where He wished to do good. And He laboured not thus for gain, for He was not smitten either with pride or with covetousness.

JOHN WYCLIFFE

There is a darkness which comes from excess of light, and then is the time to listen.

OSWALD CHAMBERS

one

The Walk to Oxford—September 1345

He had slept in fits and starts, and then wakened with finality as the first rays of morning light penetrated through a crack in the door. Hearing his parents awake, and then his siblings, John prepared himself for a hasty good-bye. A hand on his shoulder was the most he could expect from his father; a loaf of bread and a piece of cooked lamb wrapped in cloth was the unspoken farewell from his mother.

As a pig and then some chickens made their way through the door of their thatched cottage to warm themselves by the nascent fire, John Wycliffe, all of fifteen years old, left home for good. He was on his way to Oxford University to begin his training to become a parish priest. He would never return to his native Yorkshire again.

Two hundred miles to go, winding through the king's

9

forests, navigating across open fields, and jumping over puddles on treacherous muddy roads, and he would be there. Two hundred miles to lose himself in thought. There were sure to be those stretches when he might not encounter the sojourning juggler or minstrel, or be able to flee from the haranguing beggar priests.

He was short for his age and scrawny but fit nonetheless. Accustomed to walking long distances, John imagined he could reach Oxford in ten days, God willing, and the occasional peasant woman providing! After all, he had not come from a comfortable home but one of hardship. There was little he had not seen.

The son of Roger and Catherine Wycliffe, John had been born in Yorkshire, in the little "thorp" of Spreswell, a few miles southeast of the larger village of Richmond. At the time, "John" was the most popular name for a boy. As the priest in Richmond would later remind him, he bore the name of no less than twenty-two popes, all born before him! The name Wycliffe (also spelled Wyclif, Wicluf, and Wycleph), a name that means literally "the water cliff," had been common to the area for several generations, as it was used to designate a plot of land that came to be known as Wycliffe Manor. (Surnames, although uncommon in the thirteen hundreds, were used to identify, for the most part, the region of one's birth or one's occupation.)

Located a few miles from the village of Richmond, the manor or farm consisted of a small main house, where the Wycliffes lived, several cottages that housed other laborers, as well as extended family members, and a church, known as Wycliffe-on-Tees, because of its location near the River

Tees. The rocky hillsides of Yorkshire made farming crops difficult, but sheep took naturally to the terrain and the raw northern climate.

Roger and Catherine were far from prosperous, and their home reflected that status. With no chimney, the house was often filled with smoke from the ever present fire. What windows did exist were not sealed with glass but rather with greased cloth, creating a dark (and dank) atmosphere. Furniture consisted of a master bed big enough for at least four—two adults and two children—and a few benches and a kitchen table.

Despite his title as lord of the manor (and patron of the rectory), Roger was no more than a tenant farmer. He was responsible for farming the hundreds of acres—with help from his family and an assortment of laborers—and for protecting the property from Scottish marauders. Because of Yorkshire's proximity to Scotland, raiding parties were a real threat. Within the last ten years, on two occasions the Wycliffes had lost half of their sheep to Scottish thieves. Thankfully, no one had been injured; warned by smoke signals from neighboring farms, the family had fled in time to the parish church in Richmond for refuge.

Once a year, Roger paid his "rent" to a bailiff from the chief steward of the earl of Richmond—in wool, not in silver. That was as close as Roger would come to royalty, as London, the residence of the earl, was, like Oxford, more than two hundred miles away. Little did John realize, as he trod patiently toward Oxford, that he would be on speaking terms with a future earl of Richmond, John of Gaunt, and indeed would cultivate a relationship that would stymie the great minds of his day. But at age fifteen, John could imagine little beyond his humble upbringing.

The sun was just now starting to rise, and John noticed, as he usually did, the eastern faces of trees, tinged orange to greet the day. He knew now would also be the time when the farmers, roused from their sleep, were out in their fields, summoning their flocks of sheep—and making sure most had made it through the night. Being a neighbor, he knew all of the farmers around Richmond, but he squinted his eyes to see one in particular. And then he caught sight of his friend's goatskin cap pulled down over his ears, his attention riveted on his fields.

"Andrew!" John shouted, his voice echoing across the rocky hills.

The goatskin cap turned around, a smile creasing a young and ruddy face. "You haven't got too far, if you're on your way to Oxford—wherever that is." And then he began to laugh at his own teasing.

"Maybe I'll never find it," John answered with a trace of seriousness.

"Well, I was hoping I'd see you before you left. Don't suppose you'll miss the sheep enough to come back some-day." Andrew looked away for an instant and then met the eyes of his friend from earliest childhood.

"No, I don't suppose," answered John. "But I will miss a few things, like Christmas and—"

"My teasing you to death," Andrew interrupted.

"Well, I'd better be on my way for now. Good-bye, Andrew. Keep an eye on my brother, would you? Someone has to stay on the farm, after all."

"That I will—and good-bye, John."

As the friends parted, Andrew walked a ways and then turned around. "John, what were you going to say, you know, about what else you would miss?"

John looked caught off guard, but then he cleared his throat and blinked a few times to stop the tears that threatened to start. "Just that I'll miss knowing how things will be, I guess. Where I'm going I won't know what to expect at all." And then he turned toward the path he had been on and continued walking, his satchel bouncing against his hip.

For generations, English country life had been more or less predictable, and children were raised to assume things would continue as they always had. There were four seasons of the year and each season held promise, based on the necessary preparation. Winter, the season that had just begun, was known as the Michaelmas season. From September 29 through Christmas, farmers sowed wheat and rye and prepared for the greatest feast of the year. John wondered how he would spend Christmas this year at Oxford. Certainly in Yorkshire it was the time when the sheep had just been slaughtered, and families could enjoy the fruits of their labors. The season that followed was known as Lent (from Christmas to Easter) and was a time of sowing oats, barley, peas, and beans. Summer came next (from Easter to August 1, also known as Lammas), and on its heels, the short but very significant time of Harvest (from Lammas to Michaelmas).

Likewise, John knew what to expect from the family life of farmers in these late Middle Ages. First and foremost, he was raised to accept death as a natural occurrence in life.

Every day he knew might very well be his last. And as he recalled his own family life and that of nearby villagers, he knew that there were many babies who hadn't lived to see their first birthday. Almost half the babies born to peasant families died in infancy due to parasites, epidemics of smallpox and measles, and various accidents. The Wycliffes, like other families nearby, had buried their share of small wooden boxes in the nearby church cemetery.

Those babies who did survive endured a rigid protocol. For the first four months or so, babies were wrapped in swaddling clothes, strips of cloth wound around every inch of the body except the face. John could remember his younger brother's chubby red face, his cheeks looking impossibly large as his ears were bound in the cloth. Several times a day the babies would be unwrapped and washed and then rewrapped, a laborious process to John, but one he was seldom responsible for. One of John's many tasks (when he was much younger) was watching the rough-hewn wooden cradle, usually placed near the fire to keep the baby warm. When the baby fussed, he pushed the cradle in a gentle motion; when one of the pigs entered the house, or one of the pesky chickens, he kept the animals away as best he could.

Following that time and up until their seventh birthday, infant boys and girls alike were dressed in skirts or dresses. There was no reason to distinguish between the sexes, as the value of all children, up until a certain age, was the same. Then, at age seven, girls began learning the tasks of their mothers, and boys followed their fathers at work. On the sheep farm, John had, in fact, been recruited to work years earlier, as soon as he was able to walk. At just a few years old, he had been assigned his own lamb to watch, making sure it didn't stray far from its mother.

To John, his life had been inextricably entwined with the sheep—at least until several months ago.

As he looked from a hilltop down into the valley and the village of Richmond, he recalled the day when he began to take his first steps beyond Wycliffe Manor. Roger, a man of few words, had surprised John one day as they were herding the sheep. "I've decided that the manor life is not for you, John," he said.

"But I'm the oldest, Father," John said, as if it were not obvious. The oldest son in most families was considered the only heir, and the natural successor as lord of the manor. While sons who followed in the birth order could stay on the farm as laborers, most chose to go elsewhere. They could apprentice themselves to a craftsman in a nearby village, or they could go into training to become priests. Daughters were expected to marry (usually by the age of sixteen), although many did not because of the shortage of landholding males. Only daughters and sons of nobility were subject to arranged marriages, and these were often used to make economic and political alliances.

"I can see that, John," Roger shot back dryly. "What I've decided is that you'll go into the priesthood. There's no greater position than parish priest."

John knew what Roger, a staunch Roman Catholic, said was true, but he also knew what his father hadn't said. He was too small and weak to be a sheep farmer, and his younger brother was the right choice to be lord of the manor someday.

15

"I've arranged for you to begin some lessons at the church in Richmond," Roger continued. What he had said so far sounded like he had practiced this speech a few times. Looking away for an instant, his demeanor seemed to change. "Oh, I don't put much value on book learning, you know that. But to be a good priest, you have to learn more than what a sheep farmer knows. And your mother and I want you to be a good priest."

The months that followed his father's pronouncement had been filled with lessons, whenever his father could spare him, at the manor church and with the parish priest in Richmond. Years earlier John had spent some time in a "petty school" in Richmond, learning how to write his name and read, but that was the extent of his education— and that of most boys in the thirteen hundreds. Those who desired further schooling had no choice but to enter the priesthood, as John was about to do. His lessons were consumed with a basic mastery of Latin, the language of the church. At Oxford all of his lessons would be in Latin, and he was expected to be proficient.

Those months had proven to his parish priest, and to his father, that the decision to leave the manor was the right one. With an agile mind and an amazing retention of information, John had surpassed even the priest's expectations. He was pronounced ready to enter the fall term of Oxford University.

From his vantage point, John could see the buildings that made up the parish church of Richmond. Any stranger could, in fact, have easily located that landmark. In every village that was large enough to sustain a parish church, the church itself was in the very center of the village, surrounded by an ample courtyard. With a smile crossing his face, John remembered the much anticipated summer fairs held in the courtyard and the young girls who would always start to dance, singing while they twirled. The courtyard was also the site of the cemetery, and from his perch John duly noted the graves in the dark northern corner of the yard (the suicides) and those in the southern sunny patch (those who were part of the church). While he felt reassured that his brothers and sisters were in the sun, he also wondered for a fleeting moment how the priest knew exactly who belonged where.

In so many ways the parish church was more than just a spiritual meeting place, serving a myriad of functions—and all at the direction of the parish priest. The church was one part warehouse, one part safe haven, as well as the place where judicial matters were decided and offenders were housed. John smiled at the thought of being in such a position as the priest, but at the same time something tugged at his conscience. In a good-sized village such as Richmond, the priest was also one of the wealthiest citizens, collecting a tenth of every parishioner's income (mainly in corn, sheep, and grain) to support the church. From this income, the priest was supposed to assist the poor and maintain the church. This man of God, whose very words were thought to hold the secrets of life, had to lead a life above reproach.

For a few fleeting seconds John wondered how anyone could live that way. Maybe, after years of training and dedication, he could.

He would stop and say a last farewell to the parish priest in Richmond. He certainly owed him that much, but that would mean talking to most of the villagers, as well. By now the shops were open, wares of all kinds were spilling onto the tiny streets, and voices were raised in friendly bartering. There was no such thing as privacy in a small English village, and it was no exaggeration to think that everyone in Richmond knew of his plans to go to Oxford.

And now he was leaving all that he knew for a bigger village, surrendering his legacy of sheep farming for an uncertain pious future. John Wycliffe had much to learn and far to go.

two

Early Years at Oxford—1345–1348

R epent!"
John's introduction to the streets of Oxford was the unmistakable plea of a beggar priest. Wagging a bony finger at the young man, the priest, lounging on the street corner, continued.

"Aye, I can see that ye have just arrived, perhaps to begin your studies? Then we've met at precisely the right time. Before the devil has his way with your soul, young man, repent now! For just a pence, I offer cleansing of your mind, freedom from your sins, and relief from the troubles of your past." Licking his lips, the priest smiled slightly, careful not to reveal what John could guess were his few remaining yellowed teeth.

John had met such priests on his way to Oxford, but he had never met one so persuasive. Before he began his studies to be a priest he could be absolved of all sin for just a pence? The offer was tempting, he thought for a second, but then, shaking his head regretfully, John hurried down the stone-paved street. He might look like a sheep farmer's son, but he had a good head on his shoulders. At the moment he had only a few pence to his name, and those would be used for his studies.

He had been delighted with the beautiful countryside just outside the city limits of Oxford. With its hills and streams, it was perfect for hunting and fishing. The upper Thames valley was known to be a prosperous agricultural region, as well as a haven for kings and knights. What his father would have said and done upon traversing such country! But his father wouldn't have known what to make of life in a town so absorbed by one university.

For a time, Oxford had been the center of a weaving industry, but since the beginning of the fourteenth century, the university had claimed "ownership" of the village. With no separate university "quarter," almost five thousand students and villagers, including women and children, lived side by side in close proximity. At the center of Oxford, a square known as Carfax, four streets met. And on those streets were the buildings that served as academic halls with their gray-tiled roofs next to narrow shops and taverns, and next to those, stables and pig styes. Where buildings stood side by side, the second stories seemed to meet, blocking out all sunlight. Then there were the churches, the towering spires of St. Mary's and St. Frideswide's, welcoming those on a road to higher learning. The city itself was surrounded by stone walls and six gates, which were supposed to be closed every night.

Standing in the center of Carfax, John surveyed the scene. It was midmorning, and he could still see a few streams of blood running from the square into the gutters of the four thoroughfares. Every morning at dawn, butchers met in the square to slaughter their animals, a scene that brought to mind John's upbringing on the sheep farm and his familiarity with life in Richmond. The smell of animal blood reminded him of his past and the memories he had endeavored to put behind him on his travels to Oxford. Now with his thoughts very much in the present, John strained his eyes for the sign of one hall in particular that he had confirmed would be his place of lodging. It had been a long journey; he was ready to end his travels and begin his life's work.

After inquiring as to the whereabouts of Balliol Hall, John made his way to Horsemonger Street, a street aptly named since it was the site of numerous horse markets where students could sell their horses at the beginning of the school term and purchase them again at year's end. John thought to himself what a difference such an animal would have made on his ten-day journey from Yorkshire. Just beyond the stables was Balliol Hall, and at its sight, John seemed to collapse to the ground.

A grand structure, Balliol boasted a large central hall used by students for meals and for classes. Upstairs were the students' quarters, separated not by walls but by hanging fabric, with three or four students per "room." The hall had been named for one John Balliol who had resided at Balliol Castle, not far from Wycliffe Manor. A man of wealth and position, John Balliol, who was also the father of a king of Scotland, offered tuition, room, and board to six students every year as an act of penance for his sins. The one stipulation was that the students chosen must all hail from the northern country—and this year's group counted one John Wycliffe among them.

Among the first to greet John was a spare man in his early thirties who quickly introduced himself. "Welcome to Balliol," he began, looking the young man up and down and making him more uncomfortable by the second. "I'm Hugh of Corbrigge, the master of the hall."

Upon introducing himself, John was quickly ushered into the hall where his name was added to an official roll, signifying that he was now enrolled as a clerk at Oxford University, the first step toward achieving the bachelor of arts degree. Hugh then directed him toward the barber's room where he was properly tonsured. With the crown of his head neatly shaved, revealing an oval shape of skin, and his hair neatly clipped along the sides and back (and all facial hair shaved as well), John was starting to look like a true cleric.

"Now, John, it's time to purchase appropriate attire befitting your new position," Hugh said.

Looking at Hugh, John suddenly felt very shabby and unkempt. Indeed, all around him in the hall were young men his age dressed in clothes signifying their rank in society as clerks at Oxford. Hugh directed John to a tavern that sold secondhand clothing—from students who had "dropped out" of college—and soon the young clerk blended in with the rest of the initiates. The clothes he purchased would be his year-round uniform: John now wore a waist-length tunic, leggings, a robe called a cappa, and a hood made from a nameless fur. The color of the fabric depended on where one resided, but all the colors were bright, as was the style of Oxford. Unlike rural areas such as Yorkshire where farmers and peasants dressed in drab colors, city folk in Oxford looked positively gaudy by comparison.

Hugh also advised John where to purchase his books. There were taverns where he could pick up secondhand copies of Aristotle and separate books of the Bible, or he could visit secondhand-book stalls, usually located just outside of Oxford. By October 10, John had finished his preparations and was ready to attend the mass at St. Mary's that celebrated the start of the new school term.

To the students at Oxford, St. Mary's, situated in the center of the walled city, was much more than an ornate cathedral. Since the only university buildings were the halls where students lived, St. Mary's served as the courtroom of the chancellor (in the adjoining Adam de Brome Chapel, added in 1328), the seat of university government, the site of classroom disputations, and the place where all degrees were awarded. Yet, despite its many uses, St. Mary's could inspire young clerics simply by its sheer grandeur. While the Gothic cathedral boasted almost innumerable lancet windows, parapets, and ribbed arches, most commanding was its profusely decorated spire, which John craned his neck to see on this morning.

Seated in the cathedral, John gazed about in awe as the entire university body was in attendance. In the rows in front of him were gathered the masters, proctors, and the highest official, the chancellor of Oxford. Beside him on one side of the church were the other clerks; across the aisle were the monks and friars, members of the religious orders.

It was no coincidence that the "seculars," the group to which John now belonged, were separated from the "orders." Since 1167, when Henry II banned English students from attending the University of Paris—the result of the orders having taken control—Oxford had been considered a sanctuary for the seculars. There they were guaranteed a modicum of freedom of discussion and expression otherwise repressed by the stifling sanctions of the Roman Catholic doctrine and bureaucracy.

Oxford University, the oldest English-speaking university in the world, had actually been in existence since 1096. Following Henry II's ruling, international students began crossing the English Channel to receive an education, and university status was finally conferred in 1231 when Oxford was recognized as a *universitas*, or corporation. Since the thirteenth century, when relations between the students and townspeople caused frequent rioting, halls of residence such as Balliol were established to house the students. While John naturally settled in Balliol because of his scholarship, the halls or "colleges" known as University and Merton were also in existence in 1345.

But sitting in St. Mary's, John was mostly unaware of the events that had transpired and of those who had preceded him in this auspicious dwelling. As a shaft of light pierced his eye at the start of this Mass of the Holy Ghost, John felt himself transported by the words, familiar though they were. Today his heart felt lighter than at any time in his short life. He felt as if God were truly speaking to him alone.

Three days later, classes officially began.

The blaring of a horn at sunrise awakened the young men of Balliol, and a line soon formed at a trough in the court-yard. John was used to rising early, but as he splashed his face with cold water, he felt his senses awaken and a knot of anticipation form inside his stomach. Would his Latin be sufficient in the classroom? How much had he really learned from the parish priest of Richmond?

None of the new clerks had been required to pass any entrance examination or mental test of fitness. The only requirement was officially to be enrolled at a residence hall, which John had accomplished without fanfare. Now that he was enrolled, he was expected to present himself for examination, following a rigorous course of study. He had already been regaled by many a story of a country boy, insufficiently prepared, who had succumbed to the plea-sures of the tavern rather than meet the demands of an Oxford education.

And what were these demands? John would be taking what was known as the "arts course," or what might be called a core curriculum. His courses would include the subjects of grammar, arithmetic, geometry, astronomy, and music theory, with the emphasis on rhetoric, logic, and phi-losophy. Classes would be held as lectures in Latin, with most textbooks having come from the pen of Aristotle.

And what were these lectures like? The anatomy of the Oxford lecture was the key to succeeding at the esteemed institution. Known as the disputation, the lecturer began by dictating a question to the students. All students copied what was said word for word but did not answer the question—at least not yet. The teacher or master then posed what might be called "subquestions" and then further divided these into even more specific queries. Students scrambled to copy every one of these questions. At the end of the lecture, the master began by answering the last question posed and working his way back to the first question he asked. By this stair step method, every nuance of Aristotle's argument could be analyzed and understood. While Aristotle was the favored tool for disputations, books of the Bible and a text called *The Four Books of Sentences* by Peter Lombard were also popular.

And what might be asked in a disputation? There might be a question on doctrine—"Did the power of the bishops come directly from Christ or by way of intermediaries?" or "Can God create a vacuum?"—or there might be such a deceptively simple interrogatory statement as "What is the greater reward, to love or be loved?"

Students were expected to perfect the disputation method themselves, for that would be the style of their final examinations. At the end of the third year of study, students could practice being the "questionist" at lectures for beginning clerks. Nine months later, they would take the actual examination for the bachelor of arts degree, an entirely oral examination administered by four masters and attended by all levels of students who could also ask questions if they wished. If the baccalaureate candidate passed that examination, he could continue his education toward the master of arts degree, which would take another three years, followed by a similarly intense oral examination. The university then required the new "master" to stay in Oxford for two more years of "necessary regency" when he would be required to preside over disputations and perform administrative tasks.

But the process would not stop there for the best and the brightest. After the time of regency, one could concentrate on a course of study in medicine, law, or theology. Years later, John Wycliffe would obtain the bachelor of theology degree, after five more years, followed by the doctor of theology, which required another two years. And again, following successful completion of those degrees, the doctoral candidate had to stay another two years at Oxford as a lecturer before he would finally be released.

Thus, any young man who entered Oxford at age fifteen might receive a doctorate degree in his midthirties, if all went well. In 1345, records show that only one-third of the clerks would go on to earn the bachelor of arts degree, and only one-sixth would eventually become masters. John Wycliffe himself would be over forty by the time he had progressed through the ranks to achieve his doctorate degree, through no fault of his own.

As the days and months passed, John's fears were quelled as he discovered his passion for learning. While most young clerks shuddered at the prospect of leading a disputation, John seemed to revel in the process of unraveling intricate philosophical issues. His body might be unfit for heavy physical labor, but his mind was capable of the most agile twists and turns. And like young scholars before and since, he longed to be in the presence of stimulating company. Providentially, he was led to one man, among the fifteen hundred residents of Oxford, who would determine his future thinking in a powerful way.

Thomas Bradwardine was a professor of mathematics whose career was nearing an end just as John Wycliffe was beginning his. Among the first so-called mathematicians, Bradwardine was also a philosopher and theologian who incorporated religion into his mathematical disputations. One day John shyly approached the aged teacher after his class with a question.

"Do you mean that the answers to man's greatest problems cannot be found inside himself? That man cannot, with much thinking and practice, discover the answers to the most intricate mathematical puzzles?"

Bradwardine chuckled softly and rubbed his scruffy beard. He then looked at the young boy beside him and peered deeply into his eyes, as if searching for a kindred spirit. Satisfied, he clutched his walking stick and motioned John to follow him a ways. "Are you not familiar with the Scripture? What our Lord Jesus Christ said to His beloved disciple, the one also called John?"

Shaking his head timidly, John said, "Please tell me."

Then, speaking in Latin, the teacher began: "Jesus said, 'Ye have not chosen me, but I have chosen you, and ordained you, that ye should go and bring forth fruit, and that your fruit should remain: that whatsoever ye shall ask of the Father in my name, he may give it you.' "

John's steps had slowed to match those of the elderly don. After several steps, Bradwardine stopped and caught his breath.

"Do you understand what that means? We—those who believe in Jesus Christ—were chosen to receive eternal life before we were born. And on earth we were chosen to bear fruit, to understand the mysteries of mathematics, but not through our own power. Whatever understanding I possess is a gift from God."

John nodded his head numbly, but his mind was spinning. How simple the great teacher made the Scripture seem! All the parish priests he had known had gone to great lengths to cloak God's Word in mysterious ritual, sparsely quoting at mass and then delivering what always seemed like a cryptic message of a few sentences.

"I can see what I have said has taken you by surprise, my young friend," Bradwardine continued. "But I believe the answer to all mysteries, the answer to life itself, can be found solely in God's Word. More importantly, salvation can only come from the sovereign grace of God. And on that point there are many who take issue with me, and will with you, if you accept what I am saying."

His thoughts racing, John thought of the pope and the bishops and all the parish priests and beggar priests who promised forgiveness and salvation through acts of penance or money. Yes, what Bradwardine was saying was controversial, yet even to his young mind, John sensed the ring of truth in his words.

As they parted a short while later, John hoped this would be the first of many more conversations. There would be other meetings, but not as many as the young clerk would have liked. Like hundreds of others in Oxford, Thomas Bradwardine was to die in a few short months, and the cause of death would be nothing short of catastrophic.

three

The Black Death—1348–1353

The stench of decaying human and animal flesh permeated the air. Not even John's remedy of wrapping his mouth and nose with a woolen scarf seemed to work. He could still smell the wretchedness of his surroundings, he could hear the pitiful cries of the dying, and he could not block from his sight the bloodied, disfigured bodies dumped unceremoniously in common trenches a short distance from Balliol Hall.

Moreover, as one of few clerks and masters who chose to remain in Oxford, John had been pressed into duty, giving a form of last rites to the local victims of this nameless scourge. Standing beside a handful of mourners, he mumbled mechanically in Latin the words "Eternal rest give them, Lord." And away from the grave site, away from the immediate horrors, he wondered, as did his countrymen, what had caused this ghastly plague. . .and why God had allowed this to happen.

When the plague struck England in 1348, John, like most scholars of his time, recalled the words of Avicenna, an eleventh-century Islamic mathematician and philosopher. In his commentary on Aristotle, Avicenna noted that during a plague he saw that rodents living underground suddenly surfaced and appeared to act like humans would if they were drunk. But like most scholars of his time, John didn't imagine a connection between rats and this hopeless scourge that would soon claim the life of his esteemed professor Thomas Bradwardine. The answer must be found elsewhere, the great minds of the day surmised. The air must be filled with disease-bearing agents, some declared, shaking their fists, while most agreed that the problem was much more serious than that: After centuries of sin and wrongdoing, God was finally exacting His punishment on the world.

Centuries would indeed pass before scientists could pinpoint the cause of what came to be known as the Black Death. Those rats observed by Avicenna were acting so strangely because they had been bitten by, or were host to, fleas that carried the bacterial strain known as *Yersinia pestis*. Periodically, the strains of *Yersinia pestis* begin to multiply in large numbers in the digestive tract of the flea and, in particular, the rat flea. Such a situation causes a blockage, and soon the flea is near starvation. Thus, while feeding on rodents, and then humans when the supply of "secondary hosts" has diminished, this "blocked flea" then regurgitates into its victims the deadly *Y. pestis* bacteria—

and the vicious cycle begins.

And a cycle it is, since the plague is now known not to occur in isolated epidemics but in what are known as pandemics, or a series of epidemics that strike in intervals of between two and twenty years. That John Wycliffe had never seen anything like the plague was not unusual since such a pandemic might only occur once in a generation.

The plague had first been observed in medieval Europe in A.D. 541 when it was dubbed "Justinian's Plague" after the Byzantine emperor reigning at the time. Between one-fifth to one-quarter of the population south of the Alps perished in that scourge. Other plagues were duly noted as occurring from 558–561; 580–582; 588–591; and 599–600. But from roughly the year 600 to the time of Wycliffe, Europe had seen only minor outbreaks of the dreaded disease. Environmental conditions and technological advances were likely responsible for the hiatus.

From the eleventh century to the early fourteenth century, Europe experienced a time of steady growth in population. Innovations in agriculture improved the diet of the masses, and food surplus meant that fewer people had to live off the land, a harsh existence at best. At the same time, the peasant population grew due to the absence of killing disease. Such halcyon days were to be short-lived, however. From 1300 until the start of the plague, what had come to be expected was rudely taken away.

While the population continued to increase, causing the land to be overcultivated, the weather became suddenly uncooperative and cold, and wet conditions prevailed. Wet growing seasons meant rotting crops in the field and swelling rivers, which resulted in outbreaks of diphtheria and typhoid fever, especially in rural areas. At the same time animal epidemics, especially those diseases that affect cattle, were increasingly common, adding to the food shortage that had been created by the famine-like conditions.

And not only Europe was in an environmental state of flux. To the far east, the land of Genghis Khan, Mongol nomads were being forced to move their flocks west in search of new pastures, and Asian wild rodents were being forced to move as well. These rodents likely were the first carriers of the Black Death, having been brought to the Gobi Desert from the Yunan region of China by Mongol horsemen.

From the Gobi Desert across the principal east-west trade routes, the fleas and rats infected with the *Y. pestis* bacteria traveled, finally arriving in Italy, then southern France, and from there to northern Europe. And there were many stops along the way. India was reported to be decimated from the outbreak, as was Constantinople in 1347, and Egypt one year later. Merchants quickly spread the word: There were dead bodies everywhere, and those countries were in chaos.

The plague was thought to enter Messina, the thriving port of Sicily, in October 1347, and by December, deaths by the dozen were reported in southern Italy. By mid-1348 the scourge had reached Paris, and a short time later, ships carrying infected rodents and fleas docked at the Dorset port of Melcombe Regis in southwest England. Because there were so many ports of entry in England, the plague spread ruthlessly throughout the country. The plague, which arrived in London in September 1348, hit the country's largest city particularly hard. From June to September of 1349, there were reported 290 deaths per day, and eventually, the plague would go on to claim 40 percent of the city's population, a devastating toll.

In Oxford, the figures would be consistent with the rest of the country. By 1350, when the plague had wrought its greatest damage, 30 percent of the university town's population had expired. John Wycliffe, who had remained at Oxford for the entire length of the siege, would only hear rumors of what had transpired at Wycliffe Manor during this time. In truth, Wycliffe Manor was abandoned as John's family and coworkers fled to the village of Richmond. There, however, the situation was equally dire as one-third of the village's residents would become infected and die.

John did not need to imagine the scenes of devastation, or the agony of the illness itself. Six days after being bitten by a flea or rodent, blackish, gangrenous pustules would appear at the site of the bite. Victims, who were often sneezing and coughing, complained of painful swelling (at the site of their lymph nodes), and soon they would display the horrid purplish blotches called buboes, the result of subcutaneous hemorrhaging—hence the name bubonic plague. Death occurred soon after, usually caused by a heart attack.

John wanted to do something to help, something more than administer last rites and offer a modicum of comfort. And like many spiritual men and women, he wasn't alone. In London there was a movement afoot based on the simple premise that the plague would end only when people accepted the errors of their ways and acknowledged the anger of God.

The movement, whose members were known as flagellants, employed decidedly masochistic methods. Baring their backs, they marched two times daily in front of St. Paul's Cathedral, flogging themselves with knotted leather whips until streams of blood coursed down their bodies. Over their heads they wore hoods with a red cross embroidered on the back and front. While they marched they chanted, "From thy dreadful pestilence, good Lord, deliver us." They continued their marches through the waning days of the plague, causing many to believe that they, the flagellants, had been right all along.

The consensus among most people was that the church had done little, but the flagellants had done much. In Balliol Hall, the few young clerks who had stayed on would mull over the consequences of this scourge on their church and their faith late into the night, their faces illumined only by candlelight. Surely their very future would be affected by the Black Death, which had killed equally among all classes of people—peasants and nobility alike.

"Obviously the physicians could do nothing to relieve the suffering," John began, "but what could we do as mere clerks? There must be a more scientific reason for this plague, one that we simply haven't the knowledge to discern."

"Yes, but what good will that reasoning do?" questioned another clerk. "The people wanted support and comfort during the crisis, and the first to leave the villages were the parish priests! You know as well as I what that will mean for the church. The pope's very vessels abandoning the people!"

Around the room murmurs could be heard and the outward signs of discontent.

"And what of the flagellants? What effect will their movement have on the people? Will this be the beginning of the end for the church?" To these questions posed by yet another clerk, silence followed.

John thought of the beggar priests and the parish priests: Each depended on the tithes of poor and rich alike. The church had failed miserably during the plague. Now, in the aftermath of the scourge, there would be an awakening—but one that no lowly clerk at Balliol Hall could predict.

The depopulation of England (and Europe) had indeed upset the carefully controlled balance between the nobility and the peasants. While John was growing up on Wycliffe Manor, there was always an abundance of workers eager to earn a peasant's wage in exchange for room and board. But following the Black Death, the population had decreased by one-third, and workers were far from plentiful. At last those peasants who made a living as agricultural workers had a bargaining tool they had never had: themselves. There would be uprisings in the years to come, but one immediate result of the plague was an increase in wages. Wealthy landlords soon discovered that the only way to keep laborers on their estates was to pay the continually escalating rate.

The newfound confidence and wealth would have many consequences. With a few more coins in their pockets, people began to change their dress and their attitudes. Clothes became more colorful and flamboyant, with men now donning tight pantaloons and long, pointed shoes and women daring to wear plunging necklines and hairpieces. Furs were seen on both men and women, and even at Oxford the priests now wore better quality furs than before the plague. And with a few more coins, people began giving charitably as never before. Their reasoning was simple: If the church couldn't help people in crisis, they would try to do so now.

As the clerks had predicted, confidence in the Roman Catholic Church had waned, but not faith in Christianity. Besides giving to the poor and needy, many in the mid-fourteenth century made pilgrimages to various religious shrines. Most people had lost many relatives, underscoring the imminence of death in their daily lives. If death could happen at any time and for a nameless reason, they needed to be prepared. Besides, they had seen entire monasteries wiped out by the plague. It was obvious to the common man and woman that God was not just displeased with them but with the church, as well.

The people had been helpless in the face of nature, and it was a feeling none wanted to experience again. While there were those who were drawn to the world of superstitions, many would cling to their God now, a God whose omnipotence they dared not question, and await the coming Judgment Day. They had seen what they thought was the end of the world, and it was truly a miracle they had survived. Now they needed to establish a more personal relationship with God, one not based on an intermediary such as a parish priest. But how would that happen?

The blackest night had at last yielded to the first signs of dawn. Light was peeking through the clouds of the late Middle Ages.

four

Studies Resume

The fall of 1353 saw Oxford University once again in session. Its numbers were depleted for both students and faculty, but the intellectual passion was still there. John Wycliffe, who had never left, propelled himself toward the final stages of obtaining his bachelor of arts degree, finally earning the baccalaureate in 1355. To him, though, that was only the first step toward his ultimate goal of earning a doctorate degree.

As with many students, money was an overriding concern. John had benefited from a scholarship at Balliol, but that money came to an end when he earned his degree. Help soon arrived when he was elected a "probationer fellow" of Merton College, where he would be one of a small group of students who had taken their first degree. The position, which entailed no real responsibilities, was simply another scholarship that allowed him to continue to study toward the master of arts degree, while assisting in lectures and disputations at Oxford. Besides his scholarly record, there was perhaps another reason for his residence at Merton. Like Balliol, Merton had been established in the mid–thirteenth century and was named for a wealthy landowner, Walter de Merton. Since many of de Merton's estates were located in the north country of England, the scholarships were usually awarded to young men, like Wycliffe, who hailed from that region.

Unlike the time spent studying toward his bachelor's degree, which was prolonged by the Black Death, John's path toward completing his master's was short and uninterrupted. By 1360, he had achieved the master of arts degree, been ordained as a priest, and assumed a new position—as third master at Balliol College. It was another scholarship position to be sure, and one he was proud to hold, but it was to be short-lived. In 1361, when he was offered the position of rector at the church in Fillingham, in Lincolnshire, considered the "fattest" stipend at Balliol, he could not in good conscience refuse.

However, the position put John in a quandary. As rector, he would have to resign his mastership, but would he have to resign completely from his studies? As a new master, he had just embarked upon his studies toward his bachelor of theology degree. To move away from Oxford would mean abandoning his dream to become a doctor of theology, a dream, he felt, that was now within his reach. He soon discovered what many others before him, who were in similar positions, had established as precedent. From his stipend he would appoint substitute vicars to take his place at Fillingham when he could not be there—in other words, when he was studying at Oxford. That done, he was able to secure a new place to stay, this time in a rented room at Queen's College, also in Oxford. Queen's was the least populated residence and was more than willing to rent space to an already established rector and theology student. In fact, despite a short absence, John would remain at Queen's until his departure from Oxford in 1381.

The year he became rector and the next would be marked by tragedy. In 1361, the plague, considered a pandemic, resurfaced in England, wreaking havoc once again. As John rode to Fillingham, he noticed the fields had been set on fire in an effort to ward off the scourge. Again, he felt useless as a tool against the disease as he offered aloe and thyme to the sick and administered last rites to the nearly departed. This time, the plague ran its course quickly, and losses were not nearly as severe.

Then, in 1362, John received news that his father, Roger Wycliffe, had died, as well as his brother, leaving the lordship of the manor to him. There is no record that John ever returned home to Yorkshire, but there is evidence of a bitterness within him that his parents failed to understand the importance of his faith. John would later write, "If a child yield himself to meekness and poverty and flee covetousness and pride from a dread of sin and to please God. . .they [his parents] curse him because he liveth well and will teach other men the will of God to save their souls. For by so doing the child getteth many enemies among his elders, and they say that he slandereth all their noble kindred who were held true men and worshipful [honorable]." Having long ago realized that he possessed no aptitude for sheep farming, John signed over his lordship to a William Wycliffe, though it is not known what relationship William was to John. Clearly, John had set his course and committed his life to academic and spiritual pursuits.

A rare gift of sorts came to John in 1362, temporarily easing his financial woes. Oxford had submitted his name in a petition to the pope to be given additional funds, and shortly after, the pope indeed granted John what was known as a "canonry and prebend"—or a clergyman's salary. In addition to Fillingham, he would be responsible for holding services at Westbury-on-Trym, just outside the city of Bristol, and for maintaining the chancel at the church in Aust. Not surprisingly, John wondered how he would accomplish everything while maintaining his studies. And, not too surprisingly, he again followed precedent. He would use his stipend to appoint priests to take his place at Westbury and to fulfill his duties at Aust. Or would he?

After a little calculation, it became obvious that he would have little money left once he paid for other vicars to take his place. He was no longer living in Merton, after all, where his basic needs were met. He needed to make more money. Apparently, he wasn't the only theological student with such an idea. For many weeks out of the year, there would be no rector at Westbury, and the chancel at Aust would go untended, as it had for years before, thanks to another's dire financial situation.

All would have gone unnoticed were it not for the visit of the bishop of Worcester, William Whittlesey, on a certain

Sunday in 1366. When he discovered no vicar at Westbury—and none at other churches as well—he promptly terminated John's tenure and stipend. John, however, did keep his small stipend for the chancel at Aust, which he did maintain, or paid to maintain, until his death in 1384. (Whittlesey, for his efforts, was awarded the most prestigious clerical position in England, being named archbishop of Canterbury in 1368.)

That blight on John's scholarly record would be all but forgotten in the years to come. A situation was brewing that would serve to launch John Wycliffe beyond Oxford's borders and onto the national and international scene.

While the Black Death had physically decimated the Oxford community, no issue had the same effect emotionally as the constant rift between the members of orders and those students known as seculars. They still exchanged ugly looks across the aisle from each other at St. Mary's, and they still lived in separate quarters in Oxford. And lately a new feud had arisen between the orders and the administration that called for an abbreviated curriculum for the monks. They did not feel that they, as priests in training, should have to submit to the same rigorous demands as the more academically minded seculars.

Because their numbers had fallen so dramatically since the plague, a new residence hall, called Canterbury College, was formed to house them. The new college was the idea of Simon Islip, then archbishop of Canterbury. But he had a different plan for the hall, a place he hoped would be the genesis of better relations between the contentious groups. At Canterbury he hoped to achieve a mixed society made up of four monks and eight needy and deserving secular clerks. The monks would still hold the reins of power, as one monk would be named warden, leaving the seculars in an inferior position from the start. The archbishop simply assumed the situation would work because he had conceived it, and those beneath him should abide by his rules.

John Wycliffe, as a member of the seculars, was a confirmed doubter from the moment he heard of Canterbury Hall. Sitting with his close friends Alan Tonworth and William Berton in their rooms at Merton College, he shook his head in disgust. "Islip may have good intentions, but he has no idea what will happen now," John said.

"The monks will make life unbearable for the seculars—and I for one wouldn't be surprised to see bloodshed," Alan said, his voice increasing in volume.

"Just look what they've done at Oxford. They are supported by an organization that is well established, and they have an argument for every issue. Why they think they are the real church, I'll never know," William then said.

"Yes, William, if they were truly a part of Christ's church they would be unified with us. But they are hypocrites to the core!" John said vehemently.

The friends' words proved to be true. After Simon Islip had appointed the monk Henry Woodhall to be the first warden of Canterbury College, chaos erupted. The situation soon became unbearable and unlivable for all concerned, and the archbishop had no choice but to intervene. By December 1365, Islip decided to abandon the experiment altogether and make Canterbury Hall into a wholly secular residence. But now he needed to appoint a new warden, and he needed to find secular students to take the places of the original monk fellows. His choice for the new warden was none other than John Wycliffe, a decision that spurred even more discussion between the friends.

"Simon Islip has opened the door for more trouble now, I fear," John said, rubbing his hands together. "I mean, I'm not ungrateful for the position—I need the money, that is a fact—but I wonder if he is up to the task of defending himself."

"He has always been a gentle soul, a frugal and simple man for an archbishop, no less," Alan agreed. "And now he will have to present his case not only to the king but also to the administration of Canterbury Cathedral."

Again, the friends' concerns were proved valid. Before either the royal assent or church approval was given for the new arrangement at Canterbury College, Simon Islip was dead (April 26, 1366). The wheels of bureaucracy had once again turned unbearably slowly. Awaiting the appointment of a new archbishop, John continued to live at Canterbury, as did the new secular residents.

When the appointment came, the news could not have been worse for the seculars. The new archbishop, Simon Langham, would be the one monk to attain the title between the twelfth and sixteenth centuries—and he would have little sympathy with the new secular arrangement of Canterbury Hall. One year later, Langham reinstated Woodhall as warden. To the archbishop's surprise and chagrin, John Wycliffe and the other seculars chose to ignore his mandate. Langham next cut off John's income, in fact expelling him from the residence. Still, the seculars chose to remain, deciding instead to fight their case by appealing to the papal court. The seculars had found some source of revenue within the residence hall, but their legal expenses involved in mounting such a campaign would be enormous. At the same time, John chose to exchange his rectory in Fillingham for one in Ludgershall in Buckinghamshire, a much less valuable position. The trade, arranged by a broker, was typical for the time: Because Ludgershall was a much poorer parish than Fillingham, Wycliffe, as part of his deal with the broker, received the difference in cash for what he would have earned at Fillingham. Perhaps John also feared that Langham would seek to take Fillingham away from him before he could make his own choices.

By 1371, the verdict by the papal court was finally handed down, going against the seculars as predicted. But while he was on the losing side and penniless, John Wycliffe could hold his head high. At Oxford he was now an immediately recognizable figure, one identified with the secular cause, and one most particularly regarded as the chief opponent of monasticism.

By 1371, John was also an accomplished writer, having written a body of philosophical musings, all in Latin, and not yet for the common man and woman. And now he was returning to his academic roots, having tested the legal and political waters ever so briefly. He was intent on preparing for his doctoral disputation. If all went well, he would achieve in a year what few men in his time had realized.

Twenty-eight years had passed since John Wycliffe entered the gates of Oxford and made his way to Horsemonger Street, to the site of Balliol Hall. He had entered as a boy, albeit one hardened by nature and the rigors of sheep farming. Now he was forty-three years old. He was not a handsome man, with too strong a nose and deep-set eyes that seemed almost lost in their sockets. Furthermore, his stature was slight and his complexion pale, giving the perception that he was weak outside and in. Nothing could be farther from the truth.

His final disputation would be waged as a debate against one John Kenningham, the master of the Carmelite monastery near Oxford. After the disputation, a panel of masters would judge whether John had indeed given a presentation worthy of obtaining the advanced degree. To all present, John Wycliffe was representing the concerns of the seculars, and Kenningham the position of the orders. The wounds of Canterbury Hall were still fresh.

Wycliffe's task at the disputation was to make a link between God and the state of flux he saw all around him. To prepare, he reviewed what he had covered during the past twenty-eight years: the courses in logic, optics, mathematics, philosophy, and theology. He remembered his conversations with Thomas Bradwardine, recalling that mathematics led to truth, and truth was a gift from God.

That was the essence of the link: God was the source of all matter, and since God operated outside the limits of time and space, one could create a chain of light, as it were, from creation to God's mind. To Wycliffe, all that he saw that he could name or describe once existed as an idea to God. But he would take this one step further: The Bible was the appearance on earth of God's ideas. Man would have a direct link to God through the Bible.

Even though the Bible was written in Latin, Wycliffe could sense the words coming off the pages like sounds, like the voice of God speaking directly to him. Thus, all the words of the Bible were true, and it could be argued that, as in mathematics, the truth of the whole gave truth to its parts.

During the disputation, Kenningham vigorously debated these points, using examples from the Bible that he believed were not literally true. In all cases, Wycliffe had an answer for his adversary. In the end, Kenningham, ever polite, wrote, "As we might compare the starry heavens to the web of a spider, so does my reasoning differ from the opinion of my master. Truly, the impressive words of such a doctor, imposing in learning and eloquence, almost confound me, for I know neither Aristotle nor the great Augustine could speak this way though both of them have endured many opponents."

On that day in 1372, John Wycliffe was awarded the degree of doctor of theology. For the graduation ceremony at St. Mary's church, John wore special knee-high boots to distinguish him from the other masters who were shod in low slippers. In truth, the boots were an unnecessary adornment for a man who had already distinguished himself from his peers, and then some.

John Wycliffe had come to the point described by John Foxe in his well-known *Book of Martyrs*: "After he had a long time professed divinity in Oxford, and perceiving the true doctrine of Christ's gospel to be adulterate, and defiled with so many filthy inventions of bishops, sects of monks, and dark errors, and after long debating and deliberating with himself (with many secret sighs and bewailings in his mind the general ignorance of the whole world), he could no longer suffer or abide the same, he at the last determined with himself to help and to remedy such things as he saw to be wide and out of the way. But forasmuch as he saw that this dangerous meddling could not be attempted without great troubles, neither that these things, which had been so long time with use and custom rooted and grafted in men's minds, could be suddenly plucked up or taken away, he thought with himself that this matter should be done by little and little. Wherefore he, starting with small things thereby opened himself a way or means to greater matters. First he assailed his adversaries in logical and metaphysical questions. . .by these originals the way was made unto greater points, so that at length he came to touch the matters of the Sacraments, and other abuses of the church."

five

The Call of Politics

B y 1371, the influence of John Wycliffe on the medieval political world could be seen "behind the scenes" through his writings. Three years later, in 1374, the newly ordained doctor of theology would be appointed as one of seven ambassadors sent by the king of England to meet with Pope Gregory XI in Bruges, in the region then known as Flanders. But to understand the significance of his mission is to have an appreciation for the turbulent times of the fourteenth century.

Who would follow whom in the English and French monarchies would determine times of war and peace, depression and prosperity, and chaos and order. For England, the beginning of the century witnessed the rule of Edward II (1307–1327), a monarch thought by most to be weak and ineffective, and who was eventually murdered after his wife,

Queen Isabella (significantly of France), led a revolt against him.

Edward II was succeeded by his fifteen-year-old son Edward III (1327–1377), an adolescent who would grow to become an extremely capable ruler. The sense of nationalism fostered by Edward III during his reign owed much to his dispute with France, which subsequently set off what came to be known as the Hundred Years' War.

The Hundred Years' War (1337–1453, despite its name) was essentially a dispute over the rights to Gascony in southern France (since the mid–thirteenth century held by England as a fief of the French king) and over the succession to the French throne. When France's Philip the Fair died in 1314, the Capetian monarchy ceased to exist as none of the king's three sons had survived infancy. The most logical heir was none other than England's Edward III, who, because of his mother, was the grandson of Philip the Fair. To prevent England from governing France, the French aristocracy laid claim to an ancient law that the crown could not pass through a woman and appointed Philip of Valois, or Philip VI (1328–1350), a cousin of the late king, to succeed instead.

Incited to declare war, Edward III, who lived by the code of chivalry, led England to many victories, chief among them the bloody Battle of Crecy in 1346. Despite the intervening years of the Black Death, the raiding and pillaging would continue off and on for decades, straining the resources of both countries and the effectiveness of their monarchs.

By 1369, when France began showing signs of reengaging in war, Edward III was, for all intents and purposes, unfit to rule. Physically, he was able, but mentally he had lost his desire to lead or to engage in any activity except hunting. Indeed, he was to spend his remaining years as a recluse on one of his manor estates; this meant leaving the administration of the government to, at first clerical and then later, more military-minded committees.

(Edward III's condition at first posed no crisis for the future of the monarchy. His oldest son and heir, Edward IV, also known as the Black Prince, was busy laying claim to conquests in France and was thought ready to assume the throne should the need arise. When he returned to England in the early 1370s, however, he was suffering from a terminal illness from which he would die in 1376. The Black Prince's demise made plain a situation not unfamiliar to the royal line. Edward IV's son, Richard II, the likely heir to the throne, had only been born in 1367: When he at last gained the throne in 1377, he was all of eleven years old. A key supporting member in the royal family, a role desperately needed, would be filled by Edward III's second son, John of Gaunt, who would also play an important part in John Wycliffe's life.)

This new government by committee was thus faced with the dilemma of once again raising taxes to finance the prolonged war. The subject of taxation was a familiar one to almost every citizen of England and, most painfully, to those of the clergy. But at this moment the subject could not have arisen at a worse time. After years of having various popes dispense with taxation out of sympathy for the war efforts, Pope Gregory XI decided to revive the practice. The reason was simple: The Pope needed the money himself.

51

While all Englishmen served two masters, the king and the pope, the clergy were the most hard-pressed. Representing only 2 percent of the population of England (around sixty thousand altogether), the clergy also possessed large amounts of property, which may have yielded three times the income of Edward III. Those clergy most heavily taxed were certainly not the lowly parish priests, whose income barely exceeded a peasant's, but those members of the clerical hierarchy known to many as "possessioners." Despite the reprieve given the English government during the Hundred Years' War, taxation was still demanded by the pope of the English clergy. In fact, the pope held such power that at any given time he could dispose of all clerically controlled property without obtaining formal consent.

That Edward III's government wished to increase taxation on the clergy struck a nerve in ecclesiastical circles. In June 1369, the government by committee decided it needed one hundred thousand pounds to finance the new war effort—fifty thousand of which would be taken from England's clergy. Those bishops and abbots who sat in Parliament, perhaps as a delaying tactic, sought to remove the debate to the formal cleric convocations that existed at the time, to the most prominent among them—Canterbury.

That effort thwarted temporarily, a formal debate was held in Parliament in 1371, and among those present was Oxford's John Wycliffe. He was there in support of an Austin friar named John Bankin, who also held a doctorate degree from Oxford. In the matter of taxation for the war effort, the friars were siding with the seculars and not the orders, and clearly Bankin had been influenced by the most

secularly minded Wycliffe. Bankin's argument was simple—
and shocking to most in attendance. If the clergy didn't want
to pay to support the war effort, the government was within
its rights to seize church property for the common good.

As he spoke, Wycliffe nodded his head in agreement.
Later he would be quoted as saying, "Already a third and
more of England is in the hands of the pope. There cannot
be two temporal sovereigns in one country; either Edward is
king or [the pope] is king. We make our choice." For some
time, indeed ever since he returned to the pages of the Bible
to discern the truth, he had advocated returning to a time of
simplicity, a time much like the first century when the
church, stripped of its accoutrements, had as its first mission
the seeking of spiritual truth and the saving of souls.

The result of the debate was promising for the government. After a convocation was held in Canterbury, the
clergy did relent to contribute forty thousand pounds in
support of the latest episode in the Hundred Years' War.
Shortly afterward, while Gregory XI was petitioning
Edward III's government for taxes supposedly long over-
due, the pope was also not above harassing the English
clergy for more money to finance war efforts in Italy. This
time, not one penny reached the pope, setting the stage for
more battles to develop.

The two great issues between church and state in fourteenth-
century England could be summed up as follows: the taxation by the pope of the clergy and the king, and the pope's
claim to appoint to higher offices of the church (otherwise
known as the sale of church offices or "benefices"). Indeed,

the latter, along with the sale of indulgences by parish priests and others (to absolve sinners of their sins so they would escape hell), were the primary sources of revenue for the pope.

This sale of benefices had begun in 1213 after a dispute between England's King John and some monks concerning the appointment of the archbishop of Canterbury. Both king and monks had appealed to Rome, where Pope Innocent III rendered an historic decision: He alone would have the right to appoint the archbishop, a right the pope claimed literally "for all time." Angered by the pope's decision, King John proceeded to defy Rome by ordering all bishops and abbots to leave England. The pope, not one to be intimidated, banned all church services in England and went on to excommunicate England's king. The pope also encouraged the French to invade England, which would be the final straw for John. Forced to surrender to the pope, the king agreed to the pope's demands that England from then on would be held "in feud" to the pope (or service to a superior lord). In addition, John agreed to pay the pope one thousand marks annually and that if he or any of his successors reneged on that agreement, that king would lose all right to his realm.

More than one hundred years later, of what importance to the pope and to the king was the sale of church offices? With each appointment of bishop or abbot to a church office in England, the pope held the right to collect a hefty tax for the appointment. Furthermore, all bishops appointed by the pope could increase their holdings by acquiring numerous benefices themselves (to be administered by others), but they were still subject to taxation by the pope. To the king, the situation worked this way: When a bishop or abbot died or left his office, the lands and other possessions he had acquired automatically became the property of the king, to be administered to his benefit. Such a practice was known as right of *regale*, and had been accepted, albeit reluctantly, by the pope and the church.

But for the English, there was more to the pope's claim of appointing benefices than finances. The increased hostility caused by the ongoing Hundred Years' War with France had cast the pope in a dim light. Since 1305 the pope had resided in Avignon, at the time just outside the border of France, and it was suspected that monies received from benefices were going to support the armies of the enemy and not the Holy Roman Church. Until the latter years of the fourteenth century, the pope was indeed under the thumb of the Capetians and the kings of Valois, a situation that had begun quite by force.

During the thirteenth century, while the popes continued to assert their authority over European clergy, their right to control political affairs was becoming increasingly debatable. When Pope Boniface VIII (1294–1303) boasted that he could depose kings "like servants," after attempting to prevent King Philip IV of France from taxing the French clergy, the king was quick to prove him wrong. Philip hired a gang who succeeded in kidnapping the pope and plundering his treasury. Upon release, the pope was a broken man who would die three weeks later. The next pope, Clement V, a Frenchman, had no desire to meet with the same end as his predecessor. Consequently, he acquiesced to demands that the new papal city be in Avignon, and he moved there from Rome in 1305. For the next seventy years, until Gregory XI returned to Rome in 1377, ultimately setting off another debacle, French popes and cardinals would rule the Roman Catholic Church.

When king and pope worked together, as Edward III had with various popes during his reign, the alliance proved beneficial to both. However, legislation against the pope, made in 1365 by Edward III as more of a bargaining chip than an act of outrage, had not been forgotten. In 1372, however, with Edward in declining health and the government by committee weakened by dissent from within and the clergy, all estates of England unanimously voted to rekindle the previous legislation and repudiate the papal claim of feudal overlordship of England begun more than a century earlier.

Instead of the casual give and take established between king and pope, the new government—emboldened by the support of the estates and the denial of the clergy to submit to the pope's latest taxation—preferred to begin formal negotiations with the pope. An emissary of the government, a Dominican friar named John Gilbert, arrived in Avignon in September 1373 armed with four demands. Among these were that no appeals should be entertained by the pope that interfered with the king's right of *regale*; that the pope should restrain from appointing any future bishops and abbots; and that the pope should abandon his taxation plans of both king and clergy until after the war was resolved.

Gregory XI did not refuse to negotiate, nor did he offer any concessions. But the English government was not going to be satisfied with a stalemate, considering the divisions within the government and the fluctuating state of the war with France. On May 1, 1374, the pope selected Bruges as the meeting site to discuss England's complaints. The choice of Bruges (also called Brugge) was perhaps auspicious, as five years earlier the independent state of Flanders had been acquired by France. Almost three months later, on July 27, seven ambassadors, chosen by the government, departed from London. Among their number was John Wycliffe, who was listed second in importance in the group—behind the bishop of Bangor.

John clung to the railing of the ship as the vessel plunged over each assaulting wave. The voyage across the English Channel had been stormy so far, but that hadn't kept the newly appointed ambassador below. To the contrary, John wanted to experience every moment of his first sea voyage, to feel the salt on his lips, the spray on his forehead. When the boat finally docked at Calais, John was the rare passenger who hadn't wanted the voyage to end.

From Calais, the elite group was ushered into coaches pulled by horses that would take them northeast, up the coast of the North Sea, to the city of Bruges in Flanders, a distance of around sixty miles. A man used to walking long distances, John found the constant jolting of the carriage far more unsettling on his bony frame than the turbulent sea voyage—once he had found his sea legs. After two days of travel, the group arrived at their destination, and what a welcoming sight Bruges was!

Bruges was a few miles inland from the sea but, to

first-time visitors, water seemed to be everywhere. Known as the "Venice of Flanders," Bruges was laced with charming canals, with some very long ones even extending to the sea. John was also amazed at the size of this thriving medieval center of trade. Since its humble start in A.D. 200 as a Roman-Gallic settlement, Bruges had become a flourishing city of thirty-five thousand, second only in size in the region to Paris, France.

As the party rode to an inn near the Basilica of the Holy Blood and the newly erected town hall (built in 1370), John almost gasped at the beauty of Bruges in the fading sunset. The dying rays seemed to underscore the burnt orange tones of the brick buildings, colors that were mirrored in the sparkling canals. He couldn't help but notice the lovely gabled homes with their pristine gardens on the edge of the canals, reached only by bridges. He hoped he would have ample opportunity to explore this delightful city—but he also knew that his mission would be most time consuming.

The mission to Bruges was to be no simple one. For the next two years, John Wycliffe would find himself in the esteemed company of the pope's confidants and cardinals, but never the pope himself. Among the various English negotiators, John would make one important acquaintance, but not until the latter days of his stay.

John of Gaunt, the duke of Lancaster, had come to Bruges after the others to offer his assistance, and it was only natural that his and Wycliffe's paths would cross. During a break in one negotiating session, the two men found themselves seated across a long oak table from each other in a pub on Blekerstraat, among other members of their party. John Wycliffe was well aware who the distinguished gentleman was, with his knightly bearing and regal manners. But he was far too shy to introduce himself in such a gathering and sought to take his leave as soon as custom would allow.

When John of Gaunt himself rose from the table, he nodded at the Oxford doctor briefly. "Perhaps we will meet sometime in England, Doctor Wycliffe. Don't look so surprised, my good man. You, Sir, are obviously more famous than you know."

Stunned, Wycliffe struggled to answer. "You flatter me, Sir John."

Acknowledging the remark with a wave of his hand, he seemed eager to get back to business. "Well, I don't know why I'm in such a hurry to meet with those cardinals one more time. I need to get back to a place where I can be useful for a change, don't you agree? We are certainly twiddling our thumbs here in Bruges!" At that, the duke gave a loud laugh, and then turned to the men on either side of him who were now standing, as well. He had concluded his audience with John Wycliffe.

Thinking about the duke's parting words, John could only surmise that even the duke's presence had failed to improve the quality of the negotiations. The bureaucracy of the papacy moved slowly, with each step of the negotiating process bogged down by minor technicalities. When a compromise was indeed reached, the result was a weak one at that. The pope and king were left with equal power over the delegation of benefices in England, with the pope giving his assurance that he would not exercise such a right in the future. John Wycliffe was well aware of the pope's careful wording: The pope, after all, had not renounced his right to benefices.

As usual, there were to be claims of betrayal among the English delegation. Soon after taking part in the negotiations, the bishop of Bangor was promoted to bishop of Hereford by none other than the pope himself.

Prior to leaving for Bruges, John himself had been awarded—by the king, not the pope—a new position as rector of Lutterworth, forcing him to give up his position at Ludgershall soon afterward. The new position was of benefit in one important way: It was equal, financially, to his previous position at Fillingham, or three times more valuable than Ludgershall. Furthermore, the position was a reward of sorts from the government. John had established a certain skill as a speaker—with talks—and the position was likely a token of appreciation for his support of antipapal measures.

While John was anxious to return to Oxford, he spent his last few days in Bruges the way he had wanted from his first day there. As he walked the winding streets that outlined the canals, he was determined to see another side of the city. He had passed prosperous citizens, noting the richness of their furs and the delicacy of the lace on men's shirts and women's shawls. Among many other exports, Bruges was known for its lace. Still, John wanted to rub shoulders with the poor people—the people with whom he was most familiar since his youth. He smiled when he reached the numerous fish markets and saw the toothless grins of the weathered vendors, and he delighted when he happened to walk into the Beguinage, a housing community founded in 1245 for the poor. Children in little more than rags raced down the muddy alleys while their mothers bartered in the streets for an onion or a small fish.

Stopping to catch his breath, he thought about his mission and how it related to the people of England, poor people just like those who lived in the small houses of the Beguinage. They were too poor to give what little they had to support the already bursting coffers of the clergy, he thought. If only the clergy could really see these people! That would only happen when and if the bishops and priests returned to a life of simplicity; if they decided, in a remarkable turnabout, to base their ministry more on Jesus' disciples and the apostle Paul than on Pope Gregory XI. Perhaps it was time for him, the shy and humble Oxford philosopher, to speak his views. For so many years he had been resigned to a future amid only the most erudite, teaching and writing for a select few. Bruges had changed all that.

Upon his return to England, far from satisfied by his experience as ambassador, John began developing his skills as a propagandist, in a series of public lectures. Referring to the pope as "Anti-Christ," John went on to describe him as "the proud, worldly priest of Rome and the most cursed of clippers and purse-kervers." Later, writing in a tract, he went on to say that "they [the pope and his collectors] draw out of our land poor men's livelihoods and many thousand marks by the year of the king's money for sacraments and spiritual things that is cursed heresy and simony [the buying or selling of church offices], and maketh all Christendom assent and maintain his heresy."

61

Such strong words likely influenced several members of what would come to be known as "The Good Parliament," who soon met to take decisive action against the pope. Contained in the Bill of Indictment against the pope were these words: "God hath given his sheep to the Pope to be pastured and not shorn and shaven. . .therefore it would be good to renew all the statutes against provisions from Rome. . . . No papal collector should remain in England upon pain of life and limb, and no Englishman, on like pain, should become such collector or remain at the court of Rome." Gregory XI, incensed as expected, wasted no time in retaliating by appointing an Italian—the illegitimate son of an English captain in the pope's service in Italy, no less—to a prominent benefice in the Church of England.

Following his mission to Bruges, John Wycliffe, with his cutting words and fearless speech, had become something of a national hero. But to those who utter strong words in a public forum, especially against a figure such as the pope, a price is often exacted. Until now he had been sheltered by his position at Oxford and afforded some protection by the government. Help was about to arrive again, and it would come in the form of the man who had once sat across an oak table from the humble scholar, a man regarded as nothing less than a legend.

six

Into the Fire

He was described by a contemporary as "a tall spare man, well-knit and erect, as a soldier should be, a man whose conversation was reserved, having something which with an enemy would pass for haughtiness and with a friend for dignity." Many would have agreed with that assessment of John of Gaunt, and John Wycliffe would likely have added more.

To the slight, middle-aged Oxford don, John of Gaunt, duke of Lancaster, was nothing less than magnificent. A physically stunning man who stood head and shoulders above the Oxford scholar, the duke of Lancaster possessed those qualities that Wycliffe did not. He was known to be restless, proud, and often arrogant, yet he was generous to a fault, even considering his enormous wealth. A soldier's soldier, he nonetheless preferred peace to battlefield heroics, and his loyalty to his father and brother, and later, nephew, was unshakable. And in his loyalty to the throne, there lay his common bond with John Wycliffe.

Simply put, John of Gaunt wished to assert the independence of the English ruler from the "feudal overlordship" of the pope, in whatever form that occurred. To do that, he began by attacking those members of government whose interests aligned with the pope's, as well as those bishops on the receiving end of choice benefices. One of his first targets was William Wickham, a bishop who had led the first "government by committee" and seized control, as John of Gaunt thought, from the duke's ailing father, Edward III. Wickham was also known to be especially greedy, at one time being in possession of an archdeaconry and eleven canonries and prebends.

Because of his reputation as a public speaker, John Wycliffe was soon summoned by John of Gaunt to a government council. The duke wasted no time getting to the point.

"Reverend Doctor John Wycliffe, your positions have preceded you," John of Gaunt began. "Like you, I believe there should be one king ruling England, one king controlling the wealth of our nation. Those who are filling the pope's treasury—and at the same time ruling England—should be reprimanded. What say you?"

"Those who serve the church should devote themselves to the Lord's work," Wycliffe answered calmly.

"You have been boldly speaking out against the pope, or so we have heard. Now the council would appreciate your voice in this matter, in support of your government, the government of King Edward III!"

"I would be honored to be of service to my government," Wycliffe said. "The English people have the right to know which of their priests are what I would call 'Caesarean clergy,' or those who are more concerned with the work of Caesar than the Lord. A priest, or a bishop, has but one task in God's eyes: to save souls."

Gathering his humble robes around him and clasping his walking stick, Wycliffe set out for the public squares and pulpits of London where his speeches would be received by willing ears. From the Tower of London to the convent of the Blackfriars, the City of London was dotted with small parish churches that could accommodate a doctor of theology on a mission from the duke of Lancaster. Life in the late Middle Ages was consumed by drudgery, and it was the rare individual who didn't welcome the latest bout between the clerics and the government.

Beyond the eager crowds, though, the don's message had found its way to St. Paul's Cathedral, the church of the young bishop of London, William Courtenay. A supporter of Wickham's and one who held very different opinions from Wycliffe and John of Gaunt, Courtenay felt he had but one course of action. If John Wycliffe wanted a public forum, he would have it—but the reception this time would be far from friendly.

John Wycliffe was called to appear before the church superiors at St. Paul's Church in London on Thursday, February 19, 1377. He had been in majestic cathedrals such as St. Paul's before, but never when he was the sole focus of attention. As he gazed at the magnificent structure, he felt his heart in his throat. He was, he thought, a simple man who now found himself about to enter a soaring edifice that proclaimed the holiness of God—but also the excesses of the church.

Originally constructed in the seventh century, the cathedral, which dominated the City of London, had been rebuilt twice after fire ravaged its structure in 1087 and then in 1136. During the last half century, the east end of the cathedral had been constructed, as well as a chapter house and cloister, in the European Gothic style. On the outside, there was an octahedral spire that seemed to touch the clouds, surrounded at its base by parapets. From the spire there followed, going downward, the tower with lancet stained-glass windows and, at its base, flying buttresses accented by turret-like pinnacles. The building of the church with its pitched roof was decorated with parapets, pointed arches, and more stained glass. To enter the church, one ascended several steps to two massive wooden doors and then into the three-aisled nave, which extended from the entrance to the chancel.

Notwithstanding the structure, John felt his knees begin to tremble at the thought of being face-to-face with the hierarchy of the church. Chief among the panel of judges would be William Courtenay, who had arranged the "meeting" that all too soon would turn into a spectacle. The bishop of London felt he had a clear-cut case against the Oxford don, whom he deemed guilty of insubordination.

But Courtenay, whose father was an earl and whose mother was the granddaughter of King Edward I, was not expecting a battle royal. For accompanying Wycliffe into the majestic doorway of St. Paul's would be none other than John of Gaunt, four doctors of divinity (one from each of the orders), and Lord Henry Percy, the marshal of England. Percy's presence was particularly galling to the bishop, as the earl took great pains to display his silver-tipped wand of office, a sign of both ecclesiastical and civic privilege.

Among these luminaries, and amid such pomp and circumstance, John Wycliffe almost faded into the background. He was, as described in one eyewitness account, "a meager form, dressed in a long, light mantle of black cloth similar to those worn by doctors, ministers, and students in Cambridge and Oxford, with a girdle round his waist." His face, though, bore the look of a man with a mission, with "sharp, bold features, a clear, piercing eye, firmly closed lips. . .his whole appearance [was] full of great earnestness of character."

The bishops, including Courtenay, were not waiting to greet Wycliffe and entourage in the nave. They were waiting patiently in the Lady Chapel, which was beneath the great rose window, a magnificent multifaceted circle of stained glass at the extreme eastern end of St. Paul's. The church was filled to capacity, the crowds that filled the nave shouting insults or support at the men to be brought before the clerical hierarchy. Finally, Henry Percy pushed through the throngs, reaching the Lady Chapel first.

"If I had known what masteries you would have kept in the church, I would have stopped you from coming hither," declared Courtenay, clearly miffed that Wycliffe had been ushered in by such esteemed company.

At that moment John of Gaunt entered the chapel, having just heard the bishop's biting welcome. "He shall keep such masteries, though you say nay," the duke replied, a smile crossing his handsome face.

Percy made way for John Wycliffe, who was visibly unaccustomed to such jostling and harassment. His wan complexion seemed paler than usual, and he clasped his walking stick so tightly that his knuckles were white.

"Sit down, Wycliffe," said Henry Percy, wanting to make the don more comfortable. "You have many things to answer to and have need to repose yourself on a soft seat."

But for the accused to sit in the presence of his judges was too much for the bishop of London. "He must and shall stand!" exploded Courtenay. "It is unreasonable that one on his trial should sit."

John of Gaunt could not resist such an opportunity to needle the bishop even more. "Lord Percy's proposal is but reasonable," he said. "And as for you [Courtenay], who are grown so arrogant and proud, I will bring down the pride not of you alone but of all the prelacy in England!"

At that exchange the crowd burst into a roar, with those farthest away furiously trying to push their way toward the chapel.

But John of Gaunt was far from finished with his adversary. "And lest you look to your parents to save you, think again. For they will have their hands full attempting to save themselves!"

To that Courtenay replied that his faith was in a heavenly Father rather than an earthly one, which only further incited the wrath of John of Gaunt: "Rather than take such words from the bishop, I should drag him out of the court by the hair of his head!"

The roar of the crowd at once became deafening, and the masses, by sheer force of will, burst into the chapel, causing the trial to be suspended. John of Gaunt, no stranger to battle, immediately grabbed Wycliffe's arm and propelled him out of the church by another exit, followed closely by Henry Percy and the other doctors. The crowd, absorbed in the moment, did not notice their disappearance for some time.

When the dust of the moment had settled, no one seemed to notice that John Wycliffe, the accused, had said nothing. And for the next few months he fully intended to keep a low profile. He would be at his desk in Oxford, far from the madding crowds of London. For the time being, at least, he was free from prosecution.

The death of Edward III on June 1, 1377, was hardly unexpected, nor was the succession to the throne of the late monarch's grandson, Richard II, a few weeks later on June 22. For several years the boy king would rely on the counsel of his uncle John of Gaunt (who now assumed the title of Regent), and his much beloved mother, Joan of Kent. Influenced no doubt by her brother-in-law, Joan was known to be a vocal and financial supporter of John Wycliffe, and one he would need in the trying days to come.

In the early days of Richard II's reign, the king's advisers debated a question that had consumed the Parliament for some time: Could the government "detain the wealth of the kingdom"—in other words, refuse to part with gold bullion, considered the basis of a country's wealth—to finance the war efforts? Alarmed about the flow of gold going to the papal court (from taxes and the revenue of benefices), the Parliament sought the opinion of someone who had already written on this very subject.

Recently John Wycliffe had written a short pamphlet that had attracted the attention of the king's advisers. But the advisers wanted more than a pat answer from an Oxford philosopher. They needed the assurance of a man of God that Parliament would be right to stand up to the pope without incurring sin by disobedience, or worse, excommunication.

In his response to the Parliament, Wycliffe based his answer on Scripture, as well as natural reason and moral conscience. The gold was England's, he wrote, and thus was to be used in defense of the country and not in support of the pope. To those who might say that the pope was God's vice-regent, Wycliffe posed the question, "Who gave him this power?" The Oxford scholar did not find the answer in Scripture, noting that even the apostle Peter did not possess such power. "The pope should choose between apostleship and kingship," John Wycliffe said. "If he preferred to be a king, let him claim nothing of us in the character of an apostle; or if he was an apostle, he could not claim the gold." Besides, he went on, what England should give the papacy should be in the form of alms, and those should not be demanded but given only when there was a need.

"If the papacy is poor, let charity begin at home," he concluded with a flourish.

With that statement, John Wycliffe had given his detractors more than enough ammunition to begin their assault anew.

On May 22, 1377, three papal "bulls" or decrees were sent to England by Pope Gregory XI. John Wycliffe's recent writings had inflamed the papal court, causing the pope himself to write these decrees chastising this "dangerous heresy" that had sprung up on English soil. Of some fifty questionable extracts written by Wycliffe, the pope found eighteen in particular to condemn. Anathema to the pope were the Oxford don's teachings that the pope has no more power than ordinary priests to excommunicate or absolve men; that princes cannot give endowments to the church that will absolve them forever; and that Christ gave no temporal lordship to the pope, or supremacy over kings. The bulls were sent to the archbishop of Canterbury, Simon Sudbury; William Courtenay, the bishop of London; the king of England (then Edward III); and Oxford University.

The pope had no doubt likely been influenced by Adam Easton, a Benedictine monk, who would soon become a cardinal. Easton had waited a long time to silence the pen and voice of John Wycliffe. Easton had been incensed by Wycliffe's support of the seculars, especially in the Canterbury College episode, but he had bided his time, not wanting to attack the esteemed philosopher on English soil. Writing from Avignon to an abbot in England, Easton was able to obtain several copies of Wycliffe's writings that he would soon disseminate to the papal court. And, judging from the papal bulls, the pope had read enough to know exactly whom to blame.

To the pope, the bishops "were watchmen sleepily nodding at their posts," and the university (Oxford) nothing more than a "slothful husbandman allowing the tares to ripen among the grain." Despite the vitriolic language, the pope wanted the powers that be in England to know exactly what was expected of them.

To bishops Sudbury and Courtenay, the task was to prove whether John Wycliffe had indeed taught these anarchic philosophies at Oxford. If the answer was affirmative, they were to put the offender in jail "like a common thief," with the object of extorting a confession. They were then to send all documents (including the hoped for confession) to Avignon, keeping John Wycliffe in chains until they received further instructions. But that was not all. If Wycliffe somehow learned of his impending arrest and escaped, the bishops were to cite him publicly to appear before the papal court within three months. They were also to try to convince the king and Parliament that the teachings of John Wycliffe were not only false but subversive of the government. The bishops clearly had their work cut out for them.

The pope ordered the university administration to hand over Wycliffe and any disciples of his to the bishops and to see that his work be "stamped out."

King Edward III was to see that all of the above was carried out in good order.

The three papal bulls, though sent in May, did not arrive in England until November 1377, and were not received by the bishops until the middle of December. By that time, the caustic language of Gregory XI had lost some of its bite. Gone was Edward III, and soon to be gone was the pope himself. The chancellor of Oxford University was none other than Wycliffe's old friend from Merton College, Alan Tonworth, and in the spirit of Oxford he refused to be intimidated. His only action was to assign Wycliffe to his quarters in Queen's College on a voluntary basis. As for the bishops, they would wait until the new year to cite Wycliffe once again.

John Wycliffe received the first invitation in January 1378. Written on parchment, in the flowery language preferred by the archbishop, the document was evidence of the bishops' eagerness to comply with the papal bull. John was asked to appear before the bishops again at St. Paul's for a hearing on his beliefs. When he showed the document to Alan Tonworth, the chancellor had already received one himself. Tonworth's face was hidden in shadows as he sat behind his desk in the Adam de Brome Chapel at St. Mary's, a few rays of light filtering through the slim lancet windows. Still, John could sense his displeasure.

"They want to make sure you will be there," the chancellor said, shaking his head. "I don't like it, John. Why are they asking you to come to St. Paul's again—if for no other reason than to stir up the crowds and capture you, this time for good?"

"The invitation is from Simon Sudbury, not Courtenay, but no doubt Courtenay is behind it, of that I am sure," John said.

"Sudbury likes to act quickly, and he is not opposed to

using violence to accomplish his means," Tonworth added with some authority.

"Violence?" Wycliffe shuddered visibly. "How can he call himself a man of the church when he will resort to harm to silence the Scriptures?"

"What will you do, John? As long as you are at Oxford, and with John of Gaunt not far away, the bishops cannot harm you."

"I know, Alan. I won't go this time, but I cannot stop the force of the papacy for long."

John knew the mind-set of the bishops all too well. However, when the bishops received John's answer, they became more cautious than before. They would not press him to attend by force or violence, but they would not stop in their pursuit of him, either. They had taken note of his friends in high places, and they knew that whatever assignation he agreed to, his entourage would not be far behind.

A few months later, in March, John received another request from the bishops, this time for a meeting in the chapel of Lambeth Palace, the home of Simon Sudbury. Since 1200 the palace, across the River Thames from the City of London, had been the official residence of the arch-bishop of Canterbury. The name *Lambeth* means "muddy landing place," which was indicative of the location of the palace in the low-lying swampy area typical of south London. To reach Lambeth, barges were used to cross the river (the archbishop himself was relayed to and fro in his own vessel), often resulting in soiled shoes and robes for those disembarking.

When John relayed word of the meeting to John of Gaunt and others, he received help from another source: the Queen Mother herself, Joan of Kent, the widow of the Black Prince and the mother of Richard II.

The bishops, unaware of the Queen Mother's role, had planned this meeting carefully—or so they thought. Word had leaked out to the masses that at last John Wycliffe would be forced to answer for his beliefs. And the masses, on the scent of the hunted, responded accordingly. When he arrived at Lambeth Palace, they surrounded him, almost suffocating him as he proceeded to enter and make his way to the chapel. As the bishops attempted, rather halfheartedly, to settle the crowds, William Courtenay espied an unwanted visitor. Sir Richard Clifford, a confidant of John of Gaunt, was striding boldly toward the dais, his mouth slightly twitching in anticipation of the bishops' reaction.

"I have in my possession a letter," Sir Richard began, waving the parchment for all to see, "sealed with the royal seal of the Queen Mother herself, Joan of Kent!"

Loud gasps greeted the announcement from the crowd and silence from the coterie of bishops whose faces betrayed their astonishment. Simon Sudbury was the first to gather his composure and attempt, this time more seriously, to settle the crowd.

"Go on, Sir Richard, we don't have all day," Sudbury urged pompously, clearly eager to return to the business at hand. The mere mention of the Queen Mother had clearly changed the tone of the meeting. No longer could John Wycliffe be considered a despised figure when he had won the support of Joan of Kent.

" 'To the bishops who have gathered at Lambeth Palace,' " Sir Richard read, clearing his throat for extra emphasis. " 'And to all who have ears to hear: By the power vested in me by the royal throne of King Richard II, I on this day proclaim that no judgment or sentence shall be passed on the Reverend Doctor John Wycliffe.' " With a flourish, Sir Richard Clifford then handed the royal pronouncement to the bishops and, with a swirl of his robes, departed from the chapel. He knew as well as the bishops that today John Wycliffe would again walk away a free man.

Unlike the trial at St. Paul's, where Wycliffe had fled the scene in fear for his life, the conclusion of this meeting would be dignified. Calmly, John gathered his own meager robes about him, clasped his walking stick in one hand and a sheaf of papers in the other, and proceeded to confront the archbishop himself.

"Archbishop Sudbury, while I will not have the opportunity to speak today, I did want to share my beliefs with you and the other bishops. Here is my written defense, one I might say I am proud to write, and one that you may share with whomever you desire."

Sudbury, his face boiling with rage, accepted the papers and turned away in a huff. Days later, after the archbishop and William Courtenay had read the written defense, they were in the same state of mind. What would they do with John Wycliffe? Was there no way to stop his poison pen?

John Wycliffe's defense was based on one premise: The pope has no political authority, and what spiritual authority he possesses is not absolute. That meant that the pope, like the common man, could fall into sin and needed to be forgiven for his trespasses.

Wycliffe went on to say that the pope has no authority over what men own, be it land or possessions. Such possessions or money cannot be used to absolve men from their sins—in fact, priests have no power to absolve men of their sins unless such absolution is accompanied by the pardon of God.

On the matter of tithes, he claimed that they were of lesser value than the preaching of the gospel by the priests. If priests failed in their preaching, they should be denied the support of tithes. "Prelates are more bound to preach truly the gospel than their subjects are to pay tithes," Wycliffe wrote. "They are more accursed who cease from their preaching than are their subjects who cease to pay tithes even while their prelates do their office well."

Furthermore, he asserted that the Roman Catholic Church had no right to own property in England, and the misuse of such land should result in England claiming such for its own.

On the matter of excommunication—the tool of popes and priests to deny the privileges of the church—including the partaking of the sacraments and communion with the church and destining the accused to hell, Wycliffe wrote that the act itself hurts no one unless they have caused God to become angry. These words challenged the basic rights of priests and pope, and the very foundation of the church.

To say Wycliffe's defense would be challenged was like saying the sun would rise on the morrow. While the bishops had breath in their bodies, and while one vestige of the life of John Wycliffe remained, the church would seek to destroy his testimony.

Following the aborted trial at Lambeth Palace, the bishops suffered another setback, and one entirely out of their control. In 1377 Gregory XI, in a bold move, had moved the papacy back to Rome from Avignon, signaling the desire of the papacy to be rid of the dominance by the French and the persuasiveness of the Italians. The death of Gregory shortly afterward in 1378, though, left the papacy in a state of chaos, with thousands of Italians surrounding the church in Rome, demanding that the next pope be Italian.

When the terrified cardinals acquiesced to the crowd's demands, electing an Italian who took the name Urban VI, the consequences of that action were felt immediately. To the extreme displeasure of the French, Urban VI proceeded to insult the non-Italian cardinals and threatened to appoint all Italian bishops, completely ignoring the French. The cardinals could take such treatment only so long, and soon they left Rome and retreated to their former base at Avignon.

Once at Avignon, the cardinals claimed they had been forced to appoint Urban VI, and that he was not the legitimate pope. They then in a second election chose a Frenchman, Clement VII, to be pope in Avignon. There were now two popes, both of whom claimed to hold the highest office in the church. The "Great Schism" had begun, a division of the church that would last until 1417, and one that would have significant implications for John Wycliffe.

Which pope would appoint benefices in England?

Which one would receive payment of taxes? And, in John Wycliffe's case, who would hear appeals from bishops—the pope in Rome or the one in Avignon?

The claims of John Wycliffe, detailed so boldly in his defense at Lambeth Palace, began to be closely reexamined by his fellow scholars at Oxford University. What was the real power of the pope, now that there were two who claimed superiority? To Wycliffe, the whole papal system had become anti-Christian. Declaring the pope to be the man of sin who "exalteth himself above God" (2 Thessalonians 2:4), he went on to write, "forasmuch as through his [the pope's] decrees, the canonical Scriptures were vilified, nullified, utterly defaced and debased, the pope is *potissimus Antichristis*—most especially Anti-Christ."

Furthermore, what was the power of excommunication? Since the Great Schism, each pope had excommunicated the other, including his bishops, priests, and followers. The question could not help but bob to the surface: Who now was saved?

While the writings and teachings of John Wycliffe began to garner renewed support at Oxford, the bishops were left in the cold. Gone was Edward III, gone was Gregory XI and his three papal bulls, and here to stay were two popes. There was no authority of the state to appeal to, not with the reign of the boy Richard and the reins of power firmly in John of Gaunt's and the Queen Mother's grasp; there was no true authority of the church, even though England would be in Urban's camp. All the bishops could do was watch and wait—and that they would do zealously.

Perhaps due to the unsettling nature of the Great Schism, the political career of John Wycliffe was coming to a close. He had made clear his views on the papacy, and now that the institution was in a state of flux, he no longer was required to act as an advocate of the government. Still, the name John Wycliffe was not far from the thoughts of the king's council, especially when the opponents of the government were the archbishop of Canterbury and the bishop of London.

In October 1378, John was summoned to the city of Gloucester to represent the king's interests in an unusual case. Two prisoners who were housed in the Tower of London had escaped and found refuge in Westminster Abbey. Cornered by royal guards near the tomb of Edward the Confessor, one prisoner was killed in the ensuing fracas. Such an action constituted a violation of the church's rights of sanctuary, and for this, most of those involved were excommunicated by Archbishop Sudbury—a move enthusiastically supported by William Courtenay. In response, the king's council cited the abbot of Westminster, Nicholas Litlington, with contempt of court—the penalty for which was the loss of his "temporalities" or church revenues—and ordered him to appear in Gloucester. The council reasoned that the farther away from London, the better.

Although no documents exist detailing Wycliffe's arguments in support of the king, the don had discussed these issues many times before. The church could claim no sacred sanctuary since it was a place for all the people, he likely interjected. Furthermore, the act of excommunication had no meaning since the king's guards were in the act of apprehending a criminal who had a reputation as one guilty of treason—thus, they were not violating God's laws, and therefore not inciting God's wrath.

Following his appearance in Gloucester, John Wycliffe returned to his beloved Oxford, and to Queen's College, to continue his favorite pursuit of writing. He would be teaching, as well, and conducting the occasional service at Lutterworth, when he had time. There was much to be done, and who knew how many years he had left, he reasoned. He could feel the blood pounding in his head, the occasional pain running down his shoulder and left arm, and the indigestion. Still, his thoughts spilled effortlessly onto page after page after page.

seven

Toward a New Doctrine, and a New Bible

For the time being, his audience was the scholarly community at Oxford and certain clerical circles. Even though he had declared these doctrines before, John Wycliffe was a man on a mission: He needed to write his thoughts on paper.

By 1378, he had published *On the Truth of Holy Scripture, On the Church, On Indulgences,* and *On the Office of the King,* as well as numerous pamphlets. The first proclaimed his position of sole reliance on Scripture as God's Word and Law, one he had adopted many years before. But in this text, John went further, signaling his future role as Bible translator. To John, the Bible, even in the hands of the most uneducated, should be sufficient and understandable. "No man is so rude a scholar but that he may learn the words of the gospel according to his simplicity," John wrote.

On the Church was a treatise on the meaning of the word "church." He wrote fervently to dispel the notion that the word meant "prelates, priests, monks and canons and friars" or the community of all faithful believers. To Wycliffe, such a definition overlooked the doctrine of predestination, one he had adopted years earlier from his conversations with Thomas Bradwardine. Overlooking the concept of free will, Wycliffe believed that no man knew whether he was numbered among the elect, even the pope himself, "whether he be of the church or whether he be a limb of the fiend." He went on to expostulate that it was useless to pray for the dead since their fate had already been sealed long ago.

In *On Indulgences,* he waxed with evangelistic fervor as he urged his readers to serve Jesus Christ alone—and not put their trust in priests (especially beggar priests) and all members of the clergy who felt called to grant indulgences. John Wycliffe wrote, "In such infinite blasphemies is the infatuated church involved, especially by the means of the tail of this dragon—that is, the sects of the friars, who labor in the cause of this illusion, and of other Luciferian seductions of the church. But arise, O soldiers of Christ! Be wise to fling away these things, along with the other fictions of the prince of darkness, and put ye on the Lord Jesus Christ, and confide, undoubtedly, in your own weapons, and sever from the church such frauds of Antichrist, and teach the people that in Christ alone and in His law, and in His members, they should trust; that in so doing, they may be saved through His goodness, and learn above all things honestly to detect the devices of Antichrist."

Finally, in *On the Office of the King,* the scholar tackled the issue of church reform, specifically those abuses he would like to see corrected. Among these were the pursuit of worldly offices and honors, the acquiring of titles and land, and the sin of simony (the buying of benefices). Returning to his theme of simplicity, Wycliffe asserted that the clergy should be made to live like the Levites of the Bible, supported by only the alms of the faithful, surrendering all worldly possessions to the laity. Overseeing the role of bishops would be the king, who would make sure the clerics were fulfilling their spiritual roles.

Was John appealing to the government to end his dispute with the bishops once and for all? Perhaps so, but he revealed his motivation for writing these treatises to no one. Beginning in 1379, though, he began to develop a doctrine that would demand an explanation, a doctrine that would distinguish him from all other "anti-clerics," a doctrine that would earn him the label of "heretic," a heretofore unheard-of denouncement in England.

The winter of 1380–81 had been a severe one, for which John Wycliffe was surprisingly thankful. He didn't have far to walk to reach his lectures, and the forbidding weather made him all the more eager to stay in his rooms and write. His pen seemed to fly down the pages, so filled was its holder with a subject that had long troubled him.

John had been poring over certain Scriptures for a few years, those passages that dealt with what had come to be known as the Eucharist. First, John found Jesus' discourse on the "bread of life": "I am that bread of life. . . . Verily,

verily, I say unto you, Except ye eat the flesh of the Son of man, and drink his blood, ye have no life in you" (John 6:48, 53).

He then turned to Matthew's account of the Last Supper: "And as they were eating, Jesus took bread, and blessed it, and brake it, and gave it to the disciples, and said, Take, eat; this is my body. And he took the cup, and gave thanks, and gave it to them, saying, Drink ye all of it; For this is my blood of the new testament, which is shed for many for the remission of sins. But I say unto you, I will not drink henceforth of this fruit of the vine, until that day when I drink it new with you in my Father's kingdom" (Matthew 26:26–29).

What followed the reading of those passages was much contemplation. In the Bible, Jesus was speaking of Himself, but He was speaking figuratively, John reasoned. And it follows that when the priest performs the rite of the Eucharist, he is speaking figuratively, too. No, he thought, writing down his rapid thoughts, the priest is not performing a magical act that changes the bread and wine of the Eucharist into Jesus' actual flesh and blood!

What John Wycliffe was suggesting was a denial of the doctrine known as transubstantiation, part of the dogma of the Roman Catholic Church. The doctrine, which was created to explain what Jesus meant by His statements "this is my body" and "this is my blood," insisted that the word "is" be taken literally.

He began by giving lectures to students at Oxford, and soon he incorporated his thoughts into the book that he titled *On the Eucharist*. Seated typically on a tall wooden stool in a drafty lecture room, he declared, "The consecrated host which we see on the altar is neither Christ nor any part of Him but the efficacious sign of Him." Pausing for a moment to gauge the reaction of his tonsured students, he continued, "No pilgrim upon earth is able to see Christ in the consecrated host with the bodily eye, but by faith." To underscore his points, he concluded by saying, "Transubstantiation cannot be shown to have any foundation in the Word of God."

Years later, in his book *Trialogus,* a treatise on various subjects he believed were wrongfully taught in the Catholic Church, Wycliffe used three characters, as part of a classical dialogue, to argue against transubstantiation. In one scene, the character Alithia asks to be shown "from reason or Scripture that there is no identification of the bread with the body of Christ." In his answer, the character Pseudis reasons this way: "First, this bread becomes corrupt, or is eaten by a mouse. Second, the same bread is the body of Christ. Third, therefore the body of Christ does thus become corrupt, and is thus eaten. . .and thus you are involved in inconsistency."

Considering his history with the anticlerical movement, John's stance on transubstantiation was significant in another way. When priests performed the rite of the Eucharist, proclaiming the bread had become Jesus' body and the wine, Jesus' blood, the act served to exaggerate the priests' own importance. How were they, fallible men like himself, able to perform this miracle? As soon as he had come to this dangerous conclusion, John was able to make an important connection. Noting that transubstantiation had not become part of Catholic dogma until the reign of Pope Innocent III (1198–1216), he suggested that the Catholic Church return, once again, to an age of simplicity, to the faith and practice of the early Christians. To Wycliffe, transubstantiation was one more example of a faith gone awry.

But to his critics, and even some he felt had been devoted supporters, a day of reckoning was about to come. Many who had accepted wholeheartedly his antipapal outbursts could not stomach this most personal assault on their most sacred religion. A young friar who had treasured his copy of one of Wycliffe's pamphlets, writing on it, "venerable doctor, Master John Wycliffe," now amended that flattering title to "execrable seducer, Master John Wycliffe."

The first alarm would be sounded not at Lambeth Palace or St. Paul's Cathedral but at Oxford University. Alan Tonworth had resigned as chancellor in the last year and had been replaced by another old friend from John's Merton College days, William Berton. But Chancellor Berton had been no supporter of John's in recent years, and when he heard of the controversial don's latest lectures on transubstantiation, he decided the time had come to take action. Not wishing to ignite the students, or John Wycliffe's numerous friends in high places, Berton executed his plan in a clandestine manner. No one would know of the commission he was about to appoint, or when meetings would be held, save the members themselves.

A commission of twelve doctors was appointed, consisting of six friars, four seculars, and two monks, to investigate John Wycliffe's teaching. After much debate, a majority of seven found the charge of teaching false doctrine to be valid, while five voted to acquit Wycliffe. Siding with the majority, William Berton wasted no time in pronouncing judgment. There would be no private meeting where the news would be delivered with somber looks and murmuring. To the chancellor, John Wycliffe had earned the right, with his treasonous views, to have the dire pronouncement delivered in public—in a classroom filled with respectful students.

Seated once again on his stool facing his students, John turned his head at the sound of a rude knocking on the classroom door, and then the door opened to reveal a messenger from the office of the chancellor.

"Yes, what have you to say?" John asked somewhat irritated. He didn't like to be interrupted in the middle of a complicated disputation.

Clearing his throat, the messenger unfurled his paper and began to read in a sonorous voice. "To Reverend Doctor John Wycliffe from William Berton, Chancellor of Oxford University and a university commission: From this day forward, those holding, teaching, or defending Doctor Wycliffe's views on transubstantiation, including Doctor Wycliffe himself, will be penalized severely. If you or any of your students do not maintain silence on this doctrine, imprisonment, suspension from the university, and excommunication will result."

Silence and stunned expressions greeted the decree. To the students the reality seemed fantastic: Simply by listening to a lecture they might be severed from the church forever. To John Wycliffe, the reality spelled betrayal by an old friend. He had been completely unaware of such a commission, or that his views were regarded with such animosity by his colleagues.

"But you ought first to have shown me that I am in error," he protested weakly.

The messenger merely glanced down at the rolled paper and, straightening the parchment, began to read the announcement again. With just the messenger present, there would be no explanation, and there would be no justification.

When the messenger departed, silence hovered uneasily in the room. Slowly at first, and then at ever increasing speed, the students began collecting their books and making their way to the door, many bumping into each other in the process. They were embarrassed and distraught, John thought, and he could not blame them. He, too, was distraught, but that was a passing emotion. In the turmoil of the classroom one thing was clear: He would never deny his beliefs, no matter how many threats were proffered.

The snow crunched under the soles of his thin leather slippers, and under the weight of his favorite walking stick. Avoiding the glances of those he passed—surely everyone had heard of his punishment, he reasoned—he walked more deliberately than usual to his rooms at Queen's College. His thoughts were still on the commission, on the twelve men who had voted for or against him. Had the vote been close, or was it an easy victory for his former friend? And whom could he trust now that the battle lines had been drawn? Those who had supported the penalty would be analyzing everything he wrote or said in the days to come.

As he opened the door to his adjoining rooms, he had an answer to one of his queries. "Nicholas!" John exclaimed, surprised yet genuinely pleased.

"You're early today," the younger man said, not looking up from his work right away. When he did, he saw immediately that something was very wrong, though his mentor was trying hard to hide his feelings. "What is it, John? You don't look at all like yourself."

Throwing up his hands, John sank to his favorite wooden chair and proceeded to explain, offering little embellishment. None was needed for Nicholas Hereford. The new doctor of theology, and longtime protégé, wholly agreed with John's views on transubstantiation and other theological issues.

"You know what this will mean, don't you?" John peered intently at Nicholas, who then laid his pen on the table.

"Yes, I see. My future at Oxford will be in doubt, too. Those who are against you will make sure every one of us—and there are many, John, you know that—are rounded up and thrown out. Berton would probably prefer that we be drawn and quartered, but I dare say that's a bit severe."

John's face broke into a crooked grin. "If Sudbury or Courtenay were here, I'd be a bit more concerned."

"Well, back to work—that's the only thing to do, John. We're getting very close, and I've made good progress today." Nicholas proudly pointed to a stack of papers next to an open Bible.

During the last two years, they had been engaged in a unique project that they hoped would be finished within the next year. The idea had grown out of John's perspective on the Holy Scripture. Since Christians are directly responsible to God, the elder doctor reasoned, to be able to know and obey God it is essential that they read the Bible. For the last two years, John had been working on translating the entire Bible from the Latin Vulgate into English, but the task was more than he alone could accomplish. Thus, Nicholas, an able Latin and Bible scholar, was working on the Old Testament and John on the New Testament.

If they were successful, they would be the first to translate the *entire* Bible. Saint Bede (673–735), also known as the Venerable Bede, had translated the Gospel of John into Saxon, but no copies survived. That effort was followed by Alfred the Great (849–900), the king of Wessex, who translated the Ten Commandments, and two English versions of the Psalms by William Schorham and Richard Roll, done in the early years of Edward III's reign. These attempts, while noble, were not well known. John intended his English version to be available to everyone, clergy and laity, rich and poor alike.

That was another purpose of his mission: to take the Bible out of libraries and monasteries and make it available to the people for whom it was written. So scarce were copies of the Bible that John's own church in Lutterworth did not have a copy, nor did most parish churches in England. Instead of Bibles, parish churches had books that contained the prayers of the mass and the Gospel and epistle for the day. Those larger churches that were fortunate to possess a Gospel book or a psalter kept those locked in a chest, far from the reach of ordinary worshipers. At Oxford, Merton College boasted two copies of the Bible, and the library at Queen's College had two volumes of more than nine hundred pages, which John was borrowing, as well as nine volumes of additional commentary.

Like his stance on transubstantiation, John's position on an English translation went against church decree. Since the early thirteenth century, the laity were not allowed to read the Bible by order from Rome: "We forbid the laity to possess any of the books of the Old and New Testaments, except perhaps the Psalter or Breviary for the Offices of the Hours of the Blessed Virgin, which some, out of devotion, wish to have; but having any of these books translated into the vulgar tongue we strictly forbid," said a loose translation.

John, who had survived three papal bulls, was not about to be intimidated by what he regarded as a despised imposition by an imperious and controlling pope. He described his position eloquently:

> *Christ and His Apostles taught the people in the language best known to them. It is certain that the truth of the Christian faith becomes more evident the more the faith itself is known. Therefore, the doctrine should not only be in Latin but in the common tongue, and as the faith of the church is contained in the Scriptures, the more these are known in a true sense the better. The laity ought to understand the faith, and as the doctrines of our faith are in the Scriptures, believers should have the Scriptures in a language familiar to the people, and to this end indeed did the Holy Spirit endue them with the knowledge of all tongues. If it is heresy to read the Bible, then the Holy Ghost*

*Himself is condemned who gave in tongues to the
apostles of Christ to speak the Word of God in all
languages that were ordained of God under
heaven. If Christ was so merciful as to send the
Holy Ghost to the heathen men to make them par-
takers of His blessed Word, why should it be taken
from us in this land that be Christian men? If you
deny Christ's words as heresy, then you make
Christ a heretic. If you condemn the Word of God
in any language as heresy, then you condemn God
for a heretic that spake the Word, for He and His
Word are all one: and if His Word is the life of the
world how may any Antichrist take it away from us
that are Christian men, and allow the people to die
for hunger in heresy.*

From the beginning, John had insisted on a literal
translation from Jerome's Latin Vulgate edition. Jerome
(347–419), a Bible scholar, had spent twenty-three years
working from Hebrew and Greek texts to achieve what
would become the classical Latin Bible. With his expertise
in Latin, and his years of theological training, John was
confident he was up to the task and could achieve his
desired result in a fraction of that time.

John loved picking up pages already translated and
imagining men and women in his village of Richmond reading those passages by themselves. From the Old Testament,
he was particularly moved by the story of creation told in
Genesis 1:1–8 (translated by Nicholas Hereford in Middle
English):

*In the firste made God of nougt heuene and
erthe. The erthe forsothe was veyn with ynne and
void, and derknessis weren vpon the face of the
see; and the Spiryt of God was born vpon the
watrys. And God seide, Be maad ligt; and maad is
ligt. And God sawg ligt, that it was good, and
deuydid [divided] ligt fro derknessis; and clepide
[called] ligt, day and derknessis, nygt. And maad
is euen and moru, o day.*

*Seide forsothe God, Be maad a firmament in
the myddel of waters, and dyuyde it waters from
watrys. And God made the firmament, and dyuy-
did watris that weren under the firmament from
thes that weren aboue the firmament; and it is
maad so. And God clepide the firmament, heuene.
And maad is euen and moru, the seconde day.*

What would these villagers think, what would burn in
their hearts, when they read Psalm 103?

*Blesse thou, my soule, to the Lord; and alle
thingus that withinne me ben, to his holi name.
Blesse thou, my soule, to the Lord; and wile thou
not forgete all the geldingus of hym. That hath
mercy to alle thi wickidnessis; that helith alle thin
infirmytees. That ageen bieth fro deth thi lif; that
crouneth thee in mercy and mercy coingis. That
fulfilleth in goode thingus the diseyr; shal be
renewed as of an egle thi youthe. Aftir oure synnes
he dide not to vs; ne aftir oure wickidnessis he*

94

gelde to vs. For after the heigte of heuene fro
erthe; he strengthide his mercy vpon men
dredende hym.

As he began to read Nicholas's efforts at translating the major prophets, one passage from Isaiah (53:3–8) leaped from the page. Here was a spellbinding description of the Messiah, Jesus Christ, who would come to earth several hundred years later. Here the people would see how prophecy was fulfilled, and perhaps begin to believe, as John did, that every word in the Bible was true.

And wee desereden hym, dispisid, and the
laste of me, man of sorewes, and witenede
infirmyte. And as hid his chere and dispisid,
wherefore ne wee setteden by hym. Vereli oure
sicknesses he tooc, and oure sorewes he bar; and
wee heelden hym as leprous, and smyten of God,
and mekid. He forsothe wounded is for oure wick-
idnesses, defoulid is for oure hidous giltes; the
discyplyne of our pes vp on hym, and with his
wannesse we ben heled. Alle wee as shep erreden,
eche in to his weie bowede doun, and the Lord
putte in hym the wickidness of vs alle. He is
offred, for he wolde, and he openede not his
mouth; as a shep to sleyng he shal be lad, and as
a lomb bifor the clippere itself he shal become
doumb, and he opened not his mouth.

Turning to his work on the New Testament, John quickly

found the passage in Matthew (11:28–30) that he knew would bless sheep farmers, villagers, and even the nobility. Everyone carried burdens—even esteemed doctors at Oxford University—that were too heavy for them to bear.

> *Alle ye that traueilen, and been charged, come to me, and I shal refreshe, or sulfille you. Take ye my yok on you, and lerne ye of me, for I am mylde and meke in herte; and ye schulen fynde reste to youre soulis. For my yok is softe, and my charge ligt.*

Finally, his eyes rested on the well-known verse of John 3:16:

> *Forsothe God so louede the world, that he gaf his oon bigetun sone, that ech man that bileueth in to him perische not, but haue euerlastinge lyf.*

Closing his eyes for a moment, he thought about those words. We are to believe in Jesus, he thought, not in the actual bread and wine, not in the parish priests standing at the altar, and not in church dogma that has no basis in Scripture and was set down by a pope. John Wycliffe would not take the penalty handed down by the clandestine Oxford commission like one forced to swallow an apothecary's remedy. No, he would appeal this sentence to the highest court in the land—to Parliament and to the very throne of Richard II.

eight

The End of an Alliance

J ohn sent his appeal, but he knew that Parliament would not be rushed into meeting on his account. The best he could hope for was a date many months in the future. The truth was that most of Richard II's advisers did not take the appeal seriously—with one glaring exception. Troubled, John of Gaunt immediately made plans to travel from his home at Savoy Palace to Oxford.

And where the duke of Lancaster went, his entourage would surely precede and follow him. Riding on horseback, John of Gaunt was preceded by messengers also on horseback carrying flags bearing his coat of arms, to announce his coming. The duke himself was followed by knights and wagons, should the regent require assistance of any kind. As he entered Oxford through the east gate and continued up High Street and through Carfax, onlookers gathered in number to gawk and wonder. Who in Oxford deserved such a visit? Most dignitaries went to visit the duke, not the other way around.

Their necks craning, these same onlookers, running to follow the caravan, then spied the messengers turning onto Queen's Street and slowing as they neared Queen's College. The duke, ignoring the townspeople, handed the reins of his steed to a messenger and then walked in long strides to the main door of the college.

John Wycliffe was as startled as the Oxfordians to see John of Gaunt. He owed his benefactor a great deal, but he had no idea to what he owed this visit. He would not be kept in the dark for long.

"Doctor Wycliffe, I was most interested to read your appeal to the king," the duke began as he assumed custody of one of two wooden chairs in the room. "I also availed myself of the opportunity to read the indictments delivered against you by the chancellor and his commission."

"Indictments I was given no opportunity to defend, Sir," John interjected. "The commission met without my knowledge, as I am sure you are aware."

"Yes, yes," the duke said, waving his gloved hand as if the doctor's protest were most trivial. "So, defend yourself—to me, now. Defend this stance of yours on—"

"Transubstantiation, Sir. More than one hundred years ago, the Roman Catholic Church decided that the bread and wine of the Eucharist must actually become the flesh and blood of Jesus Christ to explain Scripture. But such a feat by priests—men like you and me—is impossible, and not in accordance with the Bible. When Jesus said, 'Take, eat, this is my body,' He was referring symbolically to His impending death on the cross, not that we should perform some mysterious act."

John noticed the duke's face getting redder and redder the longer he spoke. Pounding his meaty fist on the table before him, the duke looked as if he were ready to burst. "But the Eucharist *is* a mystery, and should always remain one! How dare you presume to know such holy things that only God knows? How dare you deny this most sacred rite!"

Though he tried again to present his position to the duke, John soon realized that his efforts were futile. The Oxford theologian had gone too far this time, and no cogent argument would convince John of Gaunt, an old-fashioned knight of the realm, that he was no heretic. Before the duke departed, the two men had reached a treaty of sorts. John Wycliffe promised he would not use the phrase "the substance of the bread and wine" when writing in English. He could still use the phrase, however, if he was writing in Latin to those who shared his theological background. For the duke's part, John knew he could remain at Oxford, though abiding by the strict guidelines set by the chancellor, and he would not be harmed. That is, he could stay in his rooms and write, but he could not teach and he could not share his "heretical" views with anyone.

By tacit agreement, the two men knew that their days of support for each other were over. There would be no last-minute rescues or eloquent appeals in Parliament. There would be no more parades into Oxford, with colorful flags flying. Watching the dust kick up on Queen's Street as the entourage departed, John felt resigned to his new status and yet oddly hopeful. Nicholas would be coming by later, and he would not be alone.

They arrived singly, not wanting to call undue attention to their meeting place. Nicholas Hereford came first, papers under his arm, as if this were any other day, and he would be spending the next several hours working on the Bible translation. After little over an hour, though, there were five men present in the rooms, besides John Wycliffe. They were seated in a semicircle around their mentor, who by way of greeting had described his visit by John of Gaunt.

"It was only a matter of time," John Wycliffe began, "before my support from the royalty was destined to end. Since I have known him, John of Gaunt has been concerned with the papacy and clerics only if they interfered with the political interests of England. By casting doubt on a solely religious rite, with no political purpose, I was treading on hallowed ground—and the duke, fearful, and yes, I feel rather superstitious, wanted to wash his hands of all such matters."

"You were only useful to him for a time, John," Nicholas added. "At least you can still keep writing—but I dare say the duke wouldn't approve of *Confession*."

Nicholas was speaking of the don's latest writings, which would be published in May, a few months from then. John had used the book to defend his stance on transubstantiation, and in so doing, to defend himself from the chancellor's charges.

To those present, all of whom had read various drafts of *Confession,* Nicholas's remark brought much-needed mirth to the gray surroundings. John himself felt some of the tension of the last few weeks slide away. It was good to be among friends, even if their time together might be short. To stay at Oxford was to endanger more to possible suspension and imprisonment. As he glanced at each man sitting in front of him, John felt a real bond of kinship and purpose. If and when he left, he felt assured his ideas would not be buried under threats but would somehow find a way to thrive.

Seated next to Nicholas was John Aston of Worcester, who had been a fellow at Merton College (after Wycliffe's tenure) and was known around Oxford as a mathematician and astronomer. One famous disputation of his, remembered by many, was his prediction, based on the positions of the planets, that seventy-five hundred years would pass between the Great Flood and the end of the world by fire, as recorded in the Book of Revelation. However, since meeting John Wycliffe, Aston had changed his focus. Instead of relishing discourses on astronomy, he now spent his time poring over Scripture, intent on restoring the purity and simplicity of the early church.

To John Aston's left was Philip Repingdon (or Repton), an Austin friar from Leicester who was working on his doctorate of theology. Even though he was a friar, and a member of the orders, he was overwhelmed by the truth of Wycliffe's theology. Just looking at his face, John Wycliffe thought, was enough to convince anyone of Philip's passion and sincerity. Of the group present, he alone had taken Wycliffe's teachings back home, to Leicester, where they had been well received. Leicester, only fifteen miles from

Lutterworth, where Wycliffe still held the position of rector, would prove to be a critical base in the years to come.

Lastly, there was Lawrence Steven, who was also known as "Bedeman," and Robert Rigg of Merton College. John Wycliffe wasn't sure who among them had bestowed the nickname on Lawrence, but he knew the reason why. The moniker, which means "one who prays," was fitting since Lawrence was a deeply spiritual man who spent much time on his knees. When the discussion became too entwined with doctrine, John would often turn to Lawrence to lead them in prayer.

Robert Rigg had known John since they were both young clerks, Rigg at Exeter College and John at Balliol. Since then, Robert had been a fellow at Merton and also served as bursar during the time John was on his mission to Bruges. Lately, and more significantly, he had served on the chancellor's clandestine commission, casting one of the five dissenting votes. (Within a year, and unbeknownst to any in the room, he would himself assume the title of chancellor.) He had cast his vote based on his support of John Wycliffe—but in a meeting such as this, he was one of the most accommodating, not wanting to antagonize anyone. John wondered briefly if Robert had the mental fortitude required should his views ever be harshly scrutinized.

John suddenly turned to Nicholas when he heard his name repeated, his attention having been diverted. "Yes, Nicholas? Forgive me if I seem slightly befuddled."

"How much longer do you think you will stay in Oxford? All of us are concerned for your safety, now that John of Gaunt and likely Joan of Kent have disowned you."

"When you first arrived I was thinking the same thing, Nicholas. Since you ask, I must be honest. The timing of the publication of *Confession* will likely coincide with my moving to Lutterworth. There is no way I can remain in Oxford when the chancellor reads what I have written."

The five men had been hanging on his every word, and now John noticed them turn to look at each other. "Now is the time to make plans, to leave the sanctuary of the university—which is no safe haven anymore—and go to the people. Soon Nicholas and I will have several books of the Bible translated into English. Take those books and begin to preach—in Leicester, Worcester, as far as your legs will carry you."

John Aston had a particular gleam in his eye. "People will know us when we come, for we will all be dressed alike. We will be like the first disciples, dressed poorly, so we do not appear above anyone despite our years of learning."

Again, all eyes fastened on their mentor, who was dressed, as usual, in his simple russet robes with no shoes on his feet. Dressed like John Wycliffe, they would leave soon, concentrating first on the region surrounding Leicester, all the while inviting new "preachers" to join them. As they preached, they would acquire a name to describe their movement, a name that had been used (unkindly) to describe rebels before. From this time forward, Hereford, Aston, Repingdon, Steven, and Rigg, and all who donned the russet robes of poverty, would be called Lollards—a name that means "mumblers," or, worse yet, "those who put their children to sleep."

Needless to say, the bishops of England, namely Sudbury

and Courtenay, would not be closing their eyes while the Lollards were preaching—and John Wycliffe was still living and breathing and writing.

There were other Lollards who were not at Oxford, but not many at first. One who shared many of Wycliffe's beliefs, though having arrived at them by a different path, was a Benedictine priest named John Ball.

Even without his radical message, Ball would have attracted attention by his looks alone. A tall man with a bright red beard, John Ball had left a monastery in York in the 1360s to begin itinerant preaching throughout England. His message, heard loud and clear especially by the poorer people, was this: A man should give tithes to a priest only if the priest made less than he. John Ball was outraged at the greed he witnessed in parish priests and bishops, at all levels of the Roman Catholic Church.

But, by 1381, the red-haired orator had a more overriding message, a message whose timeliness could not be denied. He began preaching that not only were all people created equal by God, but if God had wanted to create peasants, or nobles for that matter, He would surely have done so. Peasantry had been created by men as a method of oppression; God had not made peasants in the Garden of Eden. To make his message more appealing, John Ball came up with a verse that would outlive him for hundreds of years:

> *When Adam dalf, and Eve span,*
> *Who was thanne a gentilman?*

In other words, when Adam dug the earth to plant, and Eve spun thread or sewed to keep them in clothes, since they were the only people on earth, who was left to be a noble? The answer, of course, was no one. There were no nobles, and there were no peasants at the beginning of the world.

In the summer of 1381, John Ball's words were on the lips of peasants and artisans in England. By then a revolt had started, one that had its roots in the Black Death of thirty years earlier when peasants had first become empowered. Like the plague, there would be many deaths resulting from this uprising and much clamoring for answers. Who had started this rebellion, and who would pay the price for the ensuing devastation? Was God still displeased with His people, and what or who had incited His wrath?

The years following the Black Death were good ones for the peasantry of England. Because there were fewer workers, those who labored in the fields or toiled in the marketplace could demand higher wages and get them. For instance, a thresher who had made three pence for a day's work before 1349 could receive 25 percent more after the plague. But those gains were short-lived, thanks to the continuing war with France and the taxation that was required to finance the continuing conflict.

The first revolts by peasants took place midcentury in France, where peasants and townspeople, upset with the incompetence of the nobility to win the war, feared they would lose all of their newfound wealth. The result was an ugly, brutal, unorganized uprising that was ended by armies of the aristocracy. A similar situation was to develop in England in June of 1381, shortly after John Wycliffe left Oxford for good for the sanctuary of Lutterworth. What began as a brutal and unorganized effort, though, soon gained a cause worth dying for and a leader whose name would one day identify the rebellion.

By June of 1381, the war had taken a turn for the worse for the English. John of Gaunt had been defeated on French soil at St. Malo, and now the French had begun invading England. They had already captured the Isle of Wight and had set fire to the town of Hastings. To certain artisans of Essex, it was only a matter of time before French sails could be seen coming down the Thames River toward them.

There was one bright spot in all this gloom, and that was John Philipot, a wealthy Londoner, who, with his own money, had financed an effort to retake English ships and even capture some French vessels. Not one of these artisans had paid a single poll tax to Philipot, and here he was, more successful than the well-heeled armies of the duke of Lancaster! So far, Parliament (and the advisers of Richard II) had asked for three poll taxes to finance the war. So far, the artisans of Essex had paid their taxes three times—but they weren't about to pay again.

When one of the king's commissioners came to Brentwood, Essex, to collect yet another tax, the artisans refused—and drove the collectors out of town. Armed with shovels and scythes, the artisans, now joined by the peasants of Brentwood, had become an angry mob that would not be appeased. When they succeeded in beheading some men in the king's party, as well as local supporters of the king, word quickly spread.

A second riot began across the Thames River at Gravesend, followed by a third riot farther south at Canterbury. After sacking and looting Canterbury, the mob proceeded to the prison of Archbishop Sudbury at Maidstone where they set free the prisoners, among them the preacher John Ball.

Like John Wycliffe, John Ball preached ideas that were not popular with the bishops of the church, and, in fact, he had already been excommunicated. For ignoring the archbishop's repeated warnings to stop preaching, Ball had been imprisoned since April. But he had not been out of touch with the leaders of the revolt. He had written letters that had been smuggled out of jail, ending one missive with the exultation, "May God save you. Now is the time!"

Now that he was free, John Ball became the voice of the rebellion—but he was not the leader. That honor would go to an ex-soldier named Wat Tyler who was described in one chronicle as "a skilled fellow with good intelligence. . . if only it had been applied to a rightful purpose." Tyler's plan was simple: The mob must get rid of the king's advisers, including the archbishop of Canterbury, and meet only with the king. Tyler believed that Richard II, now fourteen years old, was on the side of the peasants. Wat Tyler's Rebellion had begun.

Richard II, abetted by his advisers, agreed to a meeting with Tyler at Blackheath, a meadow across the Thames from the Tower of London. Stationed in the tower, Richard and his counselors watched and waited for the mob to approach.

Meanwhile, Tyler's fragmented mobs raided prisons, releasing prisoners, and raided and pillaged Lambeth Palace. When the day of the meeting came—June 13, Corpus Christi Day—thousands had gathered on the shores of Blackheath to await the king's party.

Instead of landing on the shores, Richard II was advised to remain in his boat, rowing up and down as various leaders of the rebellion shouted to him. The rebels demanded the deaths of John of Gaunt (who was in Scotland at the time), Simon Sudbury (the archbishop of Canterbury), and William Courtenay. Wat Tyler sent his requests to the king by messenger in a small boat. After a day of trading messages, John Ball again provided the voice to the mob by preaching that night on the meadow.

William Courtenay, safely ensconced in the Tower of London, received snippets of Ball's sermon by messenger. He had, of course, heard Ball's heresies before, but only now did they relate directly to what was happening on Blackheath. Why had he not thought of this before? To Courtenay's ears, John Ball was preaching exactly what John Wycliffe had been writing about! This wasn't just a revolt against poll taxes. This was heresy put into action, and it had started years before at Oxford University. As a virtual prisoner, Courtenay could not take action right then, but the seed had been planted in his mind, and he would not forget. Wycliffe would finally pay for his heresy, he thought, strangely satisfied.

Meanwhile, in an effort to negotiate, the king sent three lesser advisers to meet with representatives of the rebels. The only bridge into London was London Bridge, and its drawbridge had been pulled up to prevent the rioters from entering the city. After receiving some assurance of peace, the drawbridge was let down—to disastrous results. The rioters poured into the city, their first destination clear. They would enter Savoy Palace and kill John of Gaunt, who they falsely assumed was there. Days later, the palace was in smoldering ruins, and many rebels had been trapped inside the inferno, many too drunk to escape from the wine cellar.

But the young king was still serious about meeting with Wat Tyler and the rebels, and a new meeting was arranged, this time at Mile End, a field northeast of London. Accompanied by his mother, Joan of Kent, the king traveled there in a carriage, while Simon Sudbury and others remained at the Tower of London. The rebels were waiting when he arrived, greeting their king with the words, "Welcome to our lord, King Richard, if it please you. We will have no other king but you."

At the meeting, Richard II made several concessions. He agreed that traitors against the king should be put to death, provided their treasonous acts could be proven by law. The king then agreed to Tyler's demand that no man should be a serf but should be paid for his work, at the rate of four pence per acre of land that he worked. He also agreed to abolish the dreaded poll tax. Hearing that, many peasants began leaving Mile End and returning to their farms, satisfied that their primary demand for an end to serfdom had been met.

However, in a short time, violence erupted again. The rebels, empowered by what they thought was their right by the king to execute traitors, dragged Simon Sudbury from the Tower of London and executed him, posting his head on London Bridge. In retaliation, Wat Tyler was then executed, with his head replacing Sudbury's on the bridge.

The death of Tyler would be the undoing of the rebellion. Within two weeks, Richard II revoked all rights he had granted at Mile End, save the abolition of the poll tax, and more leaders of the rebellion were executed in public view. The voice of the peasants, John Ball was given a weekend to recant the theological positions that had fueled this revolt, a courtesy granted by William Courtenay in deference to Ball's Benedictine training. When Ball refused he, too, was executed—in the presence of Richard II—without receiving the last rites of the church.

Shortly afterward, William Courtenay, who had managed to escape from the Tower of London, was appointed archbishop of Canterbury to succeed his friend Simon Sudbury. He had not forgotten John Ball's inflammatory words on Blackheath, nor had he forgotten his tumultuous history with the Oxford theologian who shared Ball's views. Now that he was archbishop, Courtenay saw his mission as never before: He would purge England of all heresy, and he would begin at Oxford.

nine

More Threats and More Appeals

William Courtenay needed little to spur him to action. When Parliament met in November of 1381 to express support for the king's suppression of Tyler's Rebellion, and to request Courtenay take measures to ensure that such a revolt was a thing of the past, the archbishop was ready and willing to proceed. First, though, he would need to call together a council of distinguished clerics, men who had the authority to pass judgment on the heretical views of John Wycliffe.

The gathering, which would be known as Blackfriars' Synod, was scheduled to begin on May 17, 1382, at the monastery of the Blackfriars on the western edge of London. Courtenay had taken great pains with the "guest list": Eight prelates, fourteen doctors of theology, six men who held bachelor of theology degrees, four monks, and fifteen friars would be in attendance. They would have ample authority to condemn the writings of Wycliffe, and, judging from the situation in Oxford (according to Courtenay), such condemnation would arrive not a moment too soon.

At the time, Oxford was in the middle of another clash between the seculars and the orders. The situation had deteriorated to such a degree that the orders even wrote a letter to John of Gaunt detailing the attacks on them and asking for his assistance. In a sermon delivered at St. Mary's, Nicholas Hereford, speaking for the seculars, said that any clerk who was a member of an order committed apostasy, or had abandoned his principles, by taking a degree from Oxford. In other words, the seculars wanted the orders out of the university, and they seemed to have the full support of the new chancellor, Robert Rigg. Hereford also used the pulpit to declare support for John Wycliffe, asking those listening to rise up in support of their fallen leader. Would they be so bold, Courtenay wondered, if the writings of John Wycliffe were roundly condemned by a group of his peers, and if the future of his fellow preachers was at stake?

Meanwhile, John Wycliffe, at home in Lutterworth, decided to appeal to Parliament one last time. Aware of the upcoming Blackfriars' Synod, he wanted the opportunity to present his views to a lay audience, in the hope of garnering support now that he could no longer depend on John of Gaunt. Early in the month of May, he presented seven points that he hoped would appeal to the patriotic leanings of the king's advisers rather than stir up their sense of outrage.

His first point called for a sweeping change. John Wycliffe proposed that all those who were members of orders should be released from their unnatural vows and set free to pursue a more Christian existence. "Since Jesus Christ shed His blood to free His church," John stated, "I demand its freedom. I demand that everyone may leave these gloomy walls within which a tyrannical law prevails, and embrace a simple and peaceful life under the vault of heaven."

John recognized that his second point would be more appealing to his audience. The corruptness of the church could be traced to its great wealth, he argued, and he called for the government to take possession of the property now owned by the church that rightly belonged to the king. In the same vein, in his third point he called for a new standard for tithing, saying tithes should only be given so that the priests could accomplish their duties. If priests were found to be untrustworthy, tithing should stop. "I demand that the poor inhabitants of our towns and villages be not constrained to furnish a worldly priest, often a vicious man and heretic, with the means of satisfying his ostentation, his gluttony, and his licentiousness, by buying a showy horse, costly saddles, bridles with dangling bells, rich garments and soft furs, while they see the wives and children of their neighbors dying with hunger," he stated with his most passionate voice.

In his appeal to Parliament, he went on to advocate the exclusion of the clergy from government service, the stoppage of all payments to Rome, and the confiscation of the benefices of absentee bishops and cardinals. After he finished listing his seven points, John retired again to Lutterworth, knowing he had said all he could. And while Parliament would not take official action on any of his points, William Courtenay was not likely to remain so neutral.

Twenty-four propositions, taken from John Wycliffe's writings, were presented at the Blackfriars' Synod. Nowhere did the name of John Wycliffe appear on any of the papers, which was Courtenay's intention. These were writings that were still circulating at Oxford and other places. The synod needed to condemn the content and then punish the pupils, reasoned Courtenay.

On May 21, 1382, on what would be the final day of the synod, as the distinguished guests gathered at the monastery were to decide which of the writings were heretical, if any, an act of nature froze the proceedings. Suddenly the chapter house where they were sitting began to shake wildly, and the ground moved beneath their feet. As the men raced out of the building, they heard the crashing of buildings around London and the wild screams and cries of people and animals.

With its epicenter in Kent, the earthquake of May 1382 wreaked considerable damage on the city of London. Steeples toppled off churches, smaller buildings were completely destroyed, and huge waves in the Thames River, large enough to topple ships, were recorded. Outside London, the bell tower of Canterbury Cathedral crumbled to the ground, and the building itself was considered unsafe due to large cracks.

The council at the Blackfriars' monastery now dubbed their meeting the "earthquake council." Yet this was no joking matter. How could they pronounce judgment on the writings of John Wycliffe when God had just pronounced judgment on them? To many present, God disapproved of their meeting and the only solution was to dismiss the proceedings immediately. But to others, William Courtenay in particular, the earthquake could be interpreted as a sign that God wanted them to rid the country of heresy.

"Gentlemen, do not be so hasty in your judgment," Courtenay said calmly. "While we all acknowledge God's role in the earthquake, we seem to differ as to His divine purpose. In my mind, the earthquake is yet another sign that those heresies that threaten our monasteries, indeed our very church, should be purged immediately and definitely from England."

Courtenay gazed around the room from face to face. The clerics' brows were deeply furrowed, their expressions deadly serious, as they listened intently to him. The archbishop knew he had them in the palm of his hand, and with a few more sentences, a few more appropriate words aptly placed, they would be quick to indict John Wycliffe.

"Consider where our priests and bishops are being trained. . .Oxford University. Now consider who has been teaching them of late: none other than the Reverend Doctor John Wycliffe, until recently, and now his many protégés. Rest assured they are ever eager to spread their heretical ideas throughout the monasteries and churches of England. And what will happen then, gentlemen? More chaos, more uprisings from the peasants, and more earthquakes!"

The distinguished theological scholars, while still serious, stared back at William Courtenay with eyes aflame.

They were ready to vote on Wycliffe's propositions; they were ready to condemn the person they believed to be the source of the pestilences of the fourteenth century. That evening, the theologians declared that ten of Wycliffe's twenty-four propositions were heretical, and the remaining fourteen were erroneous. Those ideas considered heretical were Wycliffe's teachings on transubstantiation and the Eucharist, the papacy, the ineffectiveness of confession, and the lack of support for property-owning clergy.

The Blackfriars' Synod also discussed the activities of what were termed "unlicensed preachers," an undisguised reference to the Lollards. To deal with these "insurgents," the council decided to appeal to the king for support on the grounds that these preachers were endangering the safety of England's citizens by stirring up dissension that could lead to another revolt. A week after the synod, the council had the royal assent, which Courtenay promptly tagged onto the incriminating statute passed by the council. Now Wycliffe's heretical ideas could neither be spread in churches nor could they be preached about in market-places, fairs, and other open spaces where people might congregate. By order of Richard II, the king's officers were authorized to arrest any unlicensed preachers and their assistants and put them in prison until the preachers had cleared themselves in an ecclesiastical court.

With the decisions clarified, and the king's order in place, William Courtenay was ready for his next move. He would publish the Blackfriars' condemnation in Oxford on June 5, on Corpus Christi Day, in the presence of the most vociferous Lollards and their would-be followers. But if the archbishop expected immediate compliance, he was in for a surprise.

Corpus Christi Day became an occasion to celebrate the end of the earthquake (and all the aftershocks that followed), the conclusion to Tyler's Rebellion, and the vanquishing of the Black Death. Certainly, God had delivered the people of England from these pestilences, and they needed to praise Him in a unique way.

All over England, plays were performed that depicted the history of humankind from the Garden of Eden to the final judgment. Traveling bands of actors traversed the country in wagons that contained the stage and various sets depicting heaven, hell, Jerusalem, and Bethlehem. The reactions of the crowd went from one extreme to another as the dramas unfolded. Oohs and aahs greeted the creation of man and woman; laughter came when Noah's wife was portrayed as too drunk to enter the ark; silence was almost palpable when the Lord stopped Abraham from killing his beloved son Isaac; and fierce anger accompanied the scene when Herod's soldiers sought to kill all baby boys following Jesus' birth.

While the high point of the drama was the crucifixion of Jesus, brought to life vividly by sound effects and the sight of real blood, the final judgment brought many closer to the church. When God appeared at the top of the wagon, separating believers from unbelievers, everyone in the audience knew where they wanted to be. They certainly didn't want to be in the company of demons, who circulated among the audience trying to woo members to follow them to hell.

In Oxford, there may have been similar plays taking place in outside venues, but inside, at St. Frideswide's, a different drama altogether was unfolding. On June 4, the day before Corpus Christi Day, Doctor Peter Stokes, a Carmelite theologian, had arrived in Oxford on a mission from William Courtenay. He had been entrusted by Courtenay to publish the Blackfriars' condemnations the next day, but he had arrived a day early. Disturbing news had come to the attention of the archbishop: Philip Repingdon, one of the original Lollards, was to be the speaker the next day at St. Frideswide's, at the invitation of Robert Rigg, the new chancellor. In fact, an entire Lollard demonstration was planned for Sunday, an event Courtenay desperately wanted to disrupt.

That Robert Rigg supported the seculars was no secret—and that he would not take orders from a Carmelite such as Peter Stokes was also well known. (Stokes, who was familiar with other Wycliffe sympathizers and had once engaged in a disputation with Nicholas Hereford, was also regarded with disdain by John Wycliffe. Seeing Stokes in his white Carmelite robes, the old Oxford don had slyly referred to him as "the white dog.") On June 4, the chancellor agreed to see Stokes in his study at St. Mary's, but the look on his face gave the archbishop's representative little confidence.

"I have for you letters from William Courtenay, the archbishop of Canterbury," Stokes began stiffly. "As you are aware, having been informed of the outcome of the Blackfriars' Synod, these letters contain the condemnation of one John Wycliffe and grant me the power to prevent the teaching of Wycliffe's heretical ideas within this university. You will note the seal of the king of England, Richard II, as well as the seals of his advisers. There is also a letter for you from the archbishop, directing me to read the statement of condemnation before Philip Repingdon delivers his sermon tomorrow."

Robert Rigg accepted the letters without looking at the messenger. He stifled a snort when he read the archbishop's letter to him, asking him to "assist our beloved son, Friar Peter Stokes, diligently, in the publication of these letters."

"Thank you for coming, Friar Stokes. I trust you will enjoy yourself during the celebration of Corpus Christi," Rigg said, his eyes betraying no emotion. "But I fear your efforts to publish such letters may be in vain. The way I see it, neither bishop nor archbishop has any power over Oxford University in matters related to heresy."

The next day, Philip Repingdon had never been more eloquent as he stood in the ornate pulpit of St. Frideswide's and spoke from his heart—and the heart of John Wycliffe. "Friends and distinguished guests, on this day of celebration we also hold up the teachings of God's servant, John Wycliffe. I believe, and I know many of you do, as well, that he has never advanced or taught any doctrine concerning the Eucharist that the Church of God has not held. He is no heretic but a man of God, most learned in the ways of the church." To much applause and cheers, Repingdon went on to condemn the mention of popes and bishops in one's prayers before lords, and he also gave credit to John of Gaunt for his continuing support—perhaps to bolster his own position.

Needless to say, Peter Stokes sat stunned in the audience. The sounds of ecstatic Lollards all around him made him fearful and anxious, and it was all he could do to keep his memory of the event intact. The archbishop wanted a full report, one ripe with details that only Stokes could provide. Following Sunday's celebration, Oxford continued the gala weekend with a series of disputations that went on for hours. Despite his tremulous demeanor, Peter Stokes was noted among the participants in one disputation.

On Monday, Peter Stokes traveled back to London to give his report to the archbishop of Canterbury. He had a vivid imagination, and he didn't want to disappoint a man as powerful as William Courtenay.

William Courtenay paced back and forth in the library of Lambeth Palace. Muttering to himself, he couldn't believe what Stokes had told him earlier that day, and then conveyed in a lengthy written report. He tried to arrange the events of the long weekend in his mind. First, there was the ridiculously unsuccessful interview with Robert Rigg, who had the gall to act as if he were above the authority of the church. Then there was the service at St. Frideswide's, where Stokes noticed twenty men sitting near him *in the church* with swords hidden under their robes!

Then, and this was the most unbelievable, there was Repingdon's sermon, where the protégé of Wycliffe urged the people to take to the streets and plunder the churches. Repingdon had even had the audacity to pretend that John of Gaunt would now protect and defend these Lollards, even though Courtenay had received good information to the contrary. Following the sermon, Stokes had witnessed Robert Rigg and Philip Repingdon laughing together—probably sharing a joke at the archbishop's expense!

While these details were fuel for the fire burning inside Courtenay, the match that had ignited the flame was one simple fact: Rigg had refused to publish the condemnations of the synod on Corpus Christi Day.

Meanwhile, Robert Rigg in Oxford had gotten wind of the grossly exaggerated, erroneous, and inflammatory report of Peter Stokes. He had only one course of action, but it was one he was loath to take. He must leave at once for London and Lambeth Palace to appeal to the archbishop. Stokes's version of the past weekend should not be allowed to stand as the absolute truth. As he was preparing to leave, Nicholas Hereford and Philip Repingdon entered his office.

"I'm off to London, to see Courtenay and settle this situation," Rigg explained tersely.

"What will you say?" asked Repingdon. "Do you regret having me preach?"

"Or was it the Lollard celebration? I cannot imagine that Courtenay will think too highly of that. Yes, what will you say?" seconded Hereford.

"No, I regret nothing that happened. Since John Wycliffe left, we have had to be bold to keep his ideas alive. But in confronting William Courtenay, my only defense is to support the independence of Oxford University. That said, it seems likely that I will have to pay a price for my supposed insubordination."

"But I did not actually advocate John's position on the

Eucharist, which is the centerpiece of the Blackfriars' condemnations," explained Repingdon.

"And Wycliffe's teachings on the Eucharist in the classroom are a thing of the past," Hereford added.

Nodding his head slowly, Rigg looked up at the two men he called colleagues and friends. He saw determination and intelligence in their eyes, but he also saw something else that he knew existed in his own heart. Fear. Would he have the courage of John Wycliffe to refuse to deny his beliefs? Or would he take the path well trod by lesser men and succumb to the archbishop's demands?

ten

Few Have Been Called

I regret to inform you that the archbishop will be unable to see you today, Doctor Rigg."

To that announcement, delivered without fanfare by the archbishop's secretary, the chancellor of Oxford was speechless. He had come as fast as he could—surely that was an indication to the archbishop of his newly repentant state of mind. Moreover, he knew the archbishop was physically in the castle, and that this refusal was part of the cleric's plan to humble the chancellor completely.

The secretary was still standing in the doorway, obviously waiting for the weary Robert Rigg to regain his composure. "However, your presence is requested by the archbishop on Thursday at the Blackfriars' monastery. Shall I convey your acceptance to the archbishop?"

The chancellor would have two more days to think

about his actions. Of course he would be at the monastery, but his mouth went dry when he considered his limited options.

On Thursday, June 12, 1382, the second meeting of the Blackfriars' Synod convened with all members present. Robert Rigg waited anxiously to be announced to the council before he entered the cavernous chamber of the monastery. Seated at the center of a long wooden table was William Courtenay, clad in the majestic robes of his office. His demeanor would match his regal bearing.

"Doctor Robert Rigg, you have been summoned to the Blackfriars' Synod to justify your actions of the weekend past," said Courtenay.

Rigg opened his mouth to speak, but he was quickly silenced by the archbishop. "You will speak only in answer to a question!" Courtenay stated, his voice rising slightly in volume. His eyes had never left Rigg.

"Were you visited by an agent of the archbishop, one Friar Peter Stokes, on Saturday past, Doctor Rigg? What say you?"

"Yes, Archbishop," Rigg answered meekly.

"And did he request that you read one document, prepared by the council and approved by King Richard II, at St. Frideswide's on the occasion of Corpus Christi Day?"

Again, Rigg answered yes.

"And did you ignore this request? Doctor Rigg, did you in good conscience interfere with the purpose of the agent of the archbishop? What say you?" The booming voice of William Courtenay echoed in the chamber, causing even a few council members to jump in their chairs.

Robert Rigg felt the color rise upward from his neck, and he wiped his brow with his sleeve. His heart beating wildly in his chest, at that moment he knew he could take no more of this inquisition. William Courtenay had the power to put him in prison and to excommunicate him. He had been foolish to suppose the Lollards could stand up to the organized church.

Flinging himself on his knees, Robert Rigg edged closer to the table. "I humbly beg your forgiveness, Archbishop! I had no right to disobey your agent, and I had no right to refuse to publish the condemnations of the council. Please, I beg of you—"

"Enough!" William Courtenay stood up from the table, glaring down at the pathetic figure of the once defiant chancellor. "I order you to return to Oxford, where you will publish the twenty-four condemnations of the Blackfriars' Synod—in Latin *and* in English. Furthermore, you are to ban the following persons from preaching or teaching at your 'esteemed' university until they have properly purged themselves of any heresy: John Wycliffe, Nicholas Hereford, Philip Repingdon, John Aston, and Lawrence Steven."

The archbishop seemed to spit out the names from his mouth, so distasteful was the mere mention of Wycliffe or any of his kindred spirits. There was, of course, no need to name John Wycliffe in that group as he had left Oxford for Lutterworth, never to return, but that wasn't sufficient for William Courtenay. In closing, the archbishop also ordered Rigg to search out those clerks and masters who were found to share the beliefs of the "heretics" and dismiss them until they, too, could be purged.

Robert Rigg was still on his face on the floor before the council. As he slowly sat back and then prepared to stand, he was stopped midway by the archbishop.

"You have sought forgiveness and will receive it, upon execution of these orders, Doctor Rigg," Courtenay said, waving in his hand the parchment documents. "Before you leave London, be aware that your presence is requested before the officers of the king. Tomorrow, at Westminster Palace, Doctor Rigg. Now, please stand, Sir. You are free to go."

Humiliated and thoroughly humbled, Robert Rigg left the monastery a changed man. He would face the king's officers the next day for further chastisement before returning to what he had once considered the safe haven of Oxford. As Robert Braybrooke, the new bishop of London, reminded him at Westminster, the chancellor would be imprisoned immediately if he failed to obey to the letter the archbishop's orders. Robert Rigg needed no more incentives.

On Sunday, June 15, 1382, the Blackfriars' condemnations were officially published at St. Mary's in Oxford by Robert Rigg himself. And later in the day, in the afternoon, the chancellor asked those cited by the archbishop to meet him in his office, also at St. Mary's. Judging from his actions in the morning, Rigg knew the men were well aware of what had transpired in London. When he told them of their suspensions and the request by the archbishop for a meeting with them, Nicholas Hereford nodded as if that was the obvious result. Now that the chancellor of Oxford could no longer be considered an ally, Nicholas would rightly assume the role of leader.

"Robert, we understand what happened and why you did what you did. But we cannot deny our beliefs without a fight. Tell me one thing: Was John of Gaunt at Westminster when you met with the king's officials?"

"No, he was not, but Nicholas—"

"That is all I needed to hear, enough for all of us," Hereford said, interrupting the chancellor.

"But you cannot approach John of Gaunt, not now anyway. He will soon hear of your suspension, and more than that, he cannot abide your stance on the Eucharist," Rigg said.

"Let us worry about the duke of Lancaster. Anyway, I do not believe he has abandoned John Wycliffe completely, and I do not believe he will turn us away."

On Monday, June 16, Nicholas Hereford and Philip Repingdon rode to Tottenhall, the new headquarters of John of Gaunt since the devastation of Savoy Palace during the peasants' revolt. The duke still had a commanding presence, but his broad shoulders seemed to sag slightly as he walked to greet the scholars. John of Gaunt had returned recently from the Scottish border where he had defeated a rebel army and negotiated a truce, squelching another assault on England. Although the gray rings around his eyes revealed his profound weariness, his speech was rapid but welcoming.

"Gentlemen, please sit down. What brings you all the way from Oxford?"

Nicholas proceeded to explain the events of Corpus Christi Day, backtracking slightly to describe the Blackfriars'

127

Synod and the twenty-four condemnations. He then described the most recent verdict of the Blackfriars and the suspensions now delivered.

"So you see, it is only a matter of time before we ourselves are called before Courtenay," Nicholas added. "We believe that our suspensions were just another step toward the ultimate control of England by the church. The power of the office of archbishop has far exceeded what it was in times past. Now with the king's consent, there is no telling what will happen to those who express slightly differing views from the church."

Before John of Gaunt could respond, Philip Repingdon wanted his say. "And we are not all that different! We are all Christians, and we all worship and love the same God. To suspend us from Oxford, which has always been a bastion of independent thinking, is to take away freedom from all of England's citizens."

John of Gaunt closed his eyes for a moment. "I hear what you are saying, and I understand your concern. William Courtenay has been no friend of mine, that is no secret. But there is still one—"

The duke was suddenly interrupted by a servant who whispered an urgent message in his ear. "It seems today is the day for visitors to descend on me," the duke said, excusing himself from Nicholas and Philip.

News had traveled quickly from Oxford to Lambeth. In another chamber of the palace, the duke greeted several emissaries of the archbishop who had come with one purpose in mind: to counter the views of the Oxford Lollards. Quietly and forcefully the visitors from Lambeth Palace reminded the duke of the Lollards' extreme position on the rite of the Eucharist. Did the duke really want to support a group of "unlicensed preachers" who questioned the fact that the bread and wine were Jesus' actual body and blood?

A short while later, the men from Oxford had their answer. The duke could not abide by all of their beliefs. In parting, he advised them to submit to the archbishop, and to do whatever necessary to purge themselves of this heresy.

Hereford and Repingdon had less than two days before their presence was required at the Blackfriars' monastery. They had lost a little of their bravado, but they were far from broken. Without the support of John of Gaunt and Robert Rigg, and without the physical presence of John Wycliffe, they would enter the lions' den alone.

The Blackfriars' council convened for a third time in the dining hall of the monastery on Wednesday, June 18, 1382, presumably to hear the pleas for forgiveness from Nicholas Hereford and Philip Repingdon. Given Robert Rigg's performance the previous week, William Courtenay had every confidence in the chancellor's powers of persuasion.

On their way to London, Nicholas and Philip had met with John Aston who was also going to present his case to the archbishop. Unlike the other two men, Aston was barefoot and clad in the russet robe of the Lollard preacher—and his mentor, John Wycliffe.

At the monastery, Hereford and Repingdon were presented first to the council. William Courtenay glared at them as he had at Rigg, but this time he sensed no imminent collapse. "Doctors Hereford and Repingdon, I present you with a copy of the twenty-four condemnations that were recently published at Oxford. What is your opinion of these condemnations?"

The two men had previously devised a plan they hoped would give them more time. "Archbishop, the condemnations you refer to require lengthy answers that we would prefer to put in writing," Nicholas said boldly.

Courtenay considered the request briefly. "Very well, gentlemen, you will have two days to prepare your answers. But be warned: These answers should not sound like an ambiguous disputation, going around and around in circles. The council requests clear, concise answers. You may go."

To John Aston, whose appearance caused council members to murmur softly, the archbishop said, "And what will you do about these condemnations? Will you discuss them in public?"

Quickly, John answered, "No, absolutely not. But neither will I stop preaching. That is what I am called to do."

Taken aback by Aston's answer, Courtenay dismissed him for two days, as well. "When you enter this room again, be prepared to explain why you should not be condemned as a heretic," he warned him sternly.

During the next two days, Hereford and Repingdon worked feverishly compiling their written answers in Latin and in English. Then they began copying their answers in English, with help from John Aston. These copies they would take to the London streets and squares. They were being accused of being heretics, and they wanted to create a sympathetic audience. Besides, they reasoned, it didn't take much to incite a London mob to action. By Friday,

June 20, the people of London were crowding into the Blackfriars' monastery, to the balcony overlooking the dining hall, to express their support of the so-called heretics.

Inwardly seething, William Courtenay would not give the crowds the victory. Acknowledging their loud and angry pleas to stop the hearing, he calmly proceeded, speaking only in Latin so the people would not understand. After having read the written responses of the two men, the council found them guilty of heresy on four counts and erroneous on two.

"I notice you have both considered most of the twenty-four condemnations to be heretical. Do you wish to recant your positions on these remaining counts, today, before this council?" asked the archbishop.

"No, we do not. We believe what we have written," answered Nicholas and Philip almost in unison.

Shaking his head slightly, the archbishop then fastened his gaze on them. "You are hereby ordered to appear at the manor house of the archbishop in Otford, Kent, one week from today for sentencing. Until then, consider your positions carefully."

The crowd had been quieted for a time, but seeing John Aston enter the hall incited them once again. Clad in the russet robe of the Lollard preacher, he smiled at the people as he entered, seemingly confident of his innocence. To each question posed by the archbishop in Latin, Aston answered defiantly in English, to the crowd's delight. To each condemnation, he answered in the most inflammatory terms. The crowd was now wild in their support, screaming insults from the rafters at the distinguished council.

Finally, the archbishop brought the third meeting of the Blackfriars to an end.

"John Aston, for your refusal to answer the condemnations in an acceptable manner, I hereby confine you to the archbishop's prison at Saltwood Castle until a date in the future. Rest assured, you will not see the light of day until you repent of this heresy!"

A week later, when Hereford and Repingdon appeared at Otford, the archbishop could not be bothered to see them. When they were again summoned to appear on July 1 in Canterbury, neither man presented himself. They had considered their positions, and they were not ready to recant.

William Courtenay could not put in prison those he could not find. But he could proceed with excommunication, and this he did with relish. The ceremony for the excommunication of Nicholas Hereford and Philip Repingdon was scheduled for Sunday, July 13, at St. Paul's Cross. The two men reacted as they had in the past. They would not sit by and do nothing. Again, Nicholas was clearly taking the lead in the matter.

"We will appeal to Rome, to Pope Urban VI, Philip," he said. "We are not heretics, and Courtenay has no right to excommunicate us."

"Both of us should not go to Rome, Nicholas. I can stay here and preach from town to town, staying out of the way of Courtenay, of course," Philip said. "You want to go, and you must. But I can keep the message alive by being here."

On July 13, while Bishop Braybrooke of London read the order of excommunication from the archbishop,

Nicholas Hereford was sailing on a boat for France. Philip Repingdon was lying low in and around Leicester, an area known to be extremely sympathetic to the Lollard cause.

The ceremony at St. Paul's Cross was stern and jarring. Standing by the cross, the bishop rang a handbell and then handed it to an acolyte. Then with a crucifix in his right hand and a candelabra in his left (with all candles lit), the bishop threw both to the ground at once. The shattering of the crucifix and candelabra signified that Hereford and Repingdon were no longer part of the church. They had indeed been severed, as the expression goes, by bell, book, and candle.

The Lollards had been evicted from Oxford and were now a scattered group. There was no telling when Nicholas would return from Rome, if ever. In England, news of the excommunication and the imprisonment of John Aston traveled quickly. How long could Philip Repingdon and Lawrence Steven remain in hiding? And, more troubling: What would William Courtenay do next?

Within a day of each other in October 1382, Lawrence Steven and Philip Repingdon presented themselves before a number of bishops and the archbishop of Canterbury himself and recanted their heretical beliefs. The life of the itinerant—and hunted—preacher was not for either of them, and both longed for the security of their past. After humbling themselves properly, Steven was reinstated as the rector of the church at Southwark and returned to Oxford to continue his studies. Repingdon also returned to Oxford where he was restored to his previous academic position, as regent-master of the university.

Delighted with these victories, William Courtenay decided to convene the next meeting of the Convocation of Canterbury at Oxford, just for good measure. To be truly rid of the heresies that had plagued England, the archbishop needed to assert his authority at the "birthplace" of the conflict—Oxford University.

The actual convocation, which would begin on November 13, 1382, with a ceremony at St. Frideswide's, was preceded by a spectacle heretofore not witnessed in Oxford. A parade from Canterbury to London and finally to Oxford was an occasion to flaunt the power of the church over the commoners and the academics. William Courtenay was joined by all the prelates and bishops of England, knights on brilliantly decorated horses, and a stream of servants. All of Oxford would recognize that the archbishop demanded and was accorded respect and reverence. Here was an archbishop who had vanquished heresy, and here were the former heretics who had seen the errors of their ways.

William Courtenay had asked Robert Rigg, as chancellor, to give the sermon on the first day of the convocation. Not coincidentally, Rigg chose as his text a verse from 2 Chronicles 20:26: "And on the fourth day they assembled themselves in the valley of Berachah; for there they blessed the LORD: therefore the name of the same place was called, The valley of Berachah, unto this day." The theme of the sermon was lost on no one listening: Like Jehoshaphat and the Jews, described in this Old Testament account, who had subdued their enemies the Ammonites, Moabites, and Edomites, William Courtenay had humbled the Oxford Lollards.

But the convocation was only beginning, and there was much more to come.

After proclaiming that the purpose of the convocation was to unearth "certain heretics" who had ties to Oxford, Courtenay then announced the formation of a committee, of which Robert Rigg would be a member, to carry out that goal long after the convocation had ended. And, speaking of those who had strayed from the dogma of the church, the archbishop then ordered Philip Repingdon to appear before all those gathered.

Repingdon would be a shining example of one who had repented of his sinful ways. While he had already recanted his supposedly heretical positions before the archbishop a month earlier, he would now give a very public testimony of that fact. "I swear by the Gospels," Philip declared, "the Gospels that I hold in my hand, never by any man's persuasion to defend or hold as true the aforesaid conclusions."

After Rigg and Repingdon, there was one more witness that William Courtenay was eager to produce before the convocation. He had been imprisoned for the past five months in a dank cell at Saltwood Castle, and he was more than ready to repent and recant. When he entered St. Frideswide's, John Aston looked like a shadow of his former self. He coughed uncontrollably, and his sickly complexion and bone-thin frame gained a measure of sympathy from the audience of his peers. But, unlike at Blackfriars' monastery, this time the crowd was silent, offering no verbal support.

Standing before William Courtenay, Aston seemed to sway from side to side as if weak from hunger. "Tell me,

John Aston, what say you now about the mystery of the bread and wine during the Eucharist?" asked Courtenay. "Would you care to expound on the teaching of the heretics in regard to that mystery?"

"I have no knowledge of that teaching," Aston answered, pleading ignorance.

Seized with a sudden pang of compassion, the archbishop then dismissed the gathering so that Aston could sit and eat—and hopefully nourish his memory as well. A plea of ignorance to the archbishop was not the same as a plea for forgiveness.

But Courtenay would not be disappointed. When he had finished eating in the dining hall of one of the residence colleges, John Aston was prepared to read a written statement in front of the large crowd of prelates and clerics. Afterward, in summary, he said, "In short, I admit to having supported the heresies of John Wycliffe, and I hereby recant my former positions. I would also like to apologize to the archbishop for my behavior at the Blackfriars' monastery last summer. Please accept my plea for forgiveness and reinstatement to the church."

Three days later, at the convocation, William Courtenay proudly forgave John Aston and reinstated him as regent-master at Oxford University. At the same time, in a final gesture, the archbishop ordered the burning of all of John Wycliffe's manuscripts so that no student then or to be enrolled could be influenced by the heretical writings.

On November 26, with all business accomplished, the Convocation of Canterbury was officially adjourned, a convocation made memorable by the outright successes of the archbishop. Oxford had been purged of all pestilence, or so thought William Courtenay. During the remaining years of the archbishop's life, there would be no plagues, peasant revolts, or earthquakes. But the ideas that had inspired the vision of John Wycliffe were still being discussed, and the man that had articulated them so forcefully was still alive, and still writing.

In November 1382, during the same month and year that the convocation was taking place, John Wycliffe surmised that he was dying.

Since his eviction from Oxford, he had filled his days writing, translating the Bible, and preaching from the pulpit of St. Mary's Church in Lutterworth. Although Lutterworth in Leicestershire was not near Oxford—more than fifty miles directly north—Wycliffe was not existing in a vacuum. He had heard that Robert Rigg, Philip Repingdon, Lawrence Steven, and John Aston had all declared him a heretic. He was saddened to hear that Nicholas Hereford, who had completed his journey to Rome, was now a prisoner in the Vatican prison, having been put away by the very man he had gone to see, Pope Urban VI. Of those he had once considered compatriots, he felt the closest to Nicholas, whom he treated like a dear brother.

Heartache and his advancing age would work against him. Sometime during November, Wycliffe collapsed from what was probably a stroke and was discovered by John Horn, a young curate at St. Mary's. He was still alive but just barely. Horn would describe his elder as "emaciated and destitute of strength" and add that he was kept alive "only by his indomitable will." Treatment for stroke consisted of rubbing a poultice of swine lard and wood sorrel on the affected body parts, as well as bleeding the patient, the most widely accepted medical remedy for any illness.

In John Wycliffe's case, there would be some permanent paralysis, and he would have difficulty walking but his spirit was intact. He would not succumb to despair—not when he was sure that his days on earth were short. Death to him, and to most fourteenth-century citizens, had always been a common and expected occurrence. The inevitable would not engulf him quite yet, though talk of his demise had become rampant.

Even the outcome of the convocation did not weaken his resolve—if anything, the result inspired righteous anger. Of the priests and prelates and archbishop who had condemned him, he wrote, "With whom, think you, you are contending? With an old man on the brink of the grave? No, with truth. Truth which is stronger than you and will overcome you."

The light that was near extinction in Oxford was still burning strongly in Lutterworth.

eleven

Dusk in Lutterworth

St. Mary's in Lutterworth, in Leicestershire, would be the first church to count among its possessions the first English translation of the entire Bible. And as rector, John Wycliffe would be the first to admit he had not accomplished the feat of translation alone. At Oxford he had worked side by side with Nicholas Hereford. When he moved to Lutterworth, he was joined in his herculean task by John Purvey.

Like John Horn, John Purvey was serving as a curate, or rector's assistant, at St. Mary's at the time of Wycliffe's retirement. Ordained a priest in 1377, Purvey was described by two contemporary chroniclers as "a most notable doctor" and "a simple chaplain." But to call him a Bible translator would be inadequate, as well. Not only would he continue and complete the English translation of the Old Testament (where Nicholas had left off), but he would also finish the New Testament for the elderly rector, as well as translate many of Wycliffe's writings and sermons into English. After the death of John Wycliffe, Purvey would launch into another English translation of the entire Bible, this time in words that were easier to understand.

To John Wycliffe, Purvey was certainly much more than a Bible translator: In truth, he was his only close companion in the final two years of his life. Dressed not like a Lollard in russet robes but like a middle-class English gentleman, Purvey would enter the rectory every morning at dawn and work until dark by candlelight. His calm demeanor and steady work habits were comforting to Wycliffe, now disabled and in frail health.

To John Wycliffe, the able curate was also the only source of news from the outside world. Upon hearing a certain morsel, the elderly man's cheeks seemed to color slightly, much to Purvey's delight.

"Tell me again, John," Wycliffe said. "I am not sure I heard you correctly."

"When Anne of Bohemia arrived for the wedding, she brought with her the usual accompaniment of servants and relatives. But also included in her party were Czech theological students who will resume their studies at Oxford." Purvey was referring to the recent royal wedding (in mid-1383) of Richard II to Princess Anne, the daughter of Bohemia's Charles IV. All of England seemed eager for details about their new queen, and Purvey chuckled at the former Oxford don's curious interest.

"And there is more, too," Purvey continued with a gleam

in his eye. "It is rumored that the princess brought three Bibles with her in three languages, no less—Latin, German, and Czech!"

Now John Wycliffe's cheeks were positively pink. "You must find a way to see her, John, soon, before she is influenced too much by the bishops and the archbishop," he said, rasping.

"What would I say to her?" Purvey questioned.

"You will simply give her our still incomplete English translation of the Bible, to add to her collection, as it were. And you will mention my name—I can only pray and hope that those theological students from Bohemia will have open minds once they reach Oxford. The church needs them, more than they will ever know."

John Purvey nodded in understanding. It was common knowledge that there were still Lollards at Oxford who met in secret to discuss Wycliffe's writings. But only with God's help would these new students ever encounter them, Purvey thought to himself.

As if reading his mind, the white-haired man sitting across the table said, "Yes, we will be in prayer about this. But in the meantime, you will go to London, won't you, John?"

Ever the obedient curate, Purvey went to London a short time later, even though with every step he took he seemed to grow more skeptical. And while he wasn't granted an actual audience with the new queen, he made sure to give parts of the new Bible to a member of the court who still respected the name of John Wycliffe. John Purvey had his doubts that Anne would receive his gift, but he wouldn't share those feelings with his beloved rector. There was too much work to be done at Lutterworth, and the curate knew as well as anyone that time was running out.

In particular, John Purvey didn't want to burden his friend with all the difficulties inherent in completing the Bible translation. Now that he had assumed most of the responsibility for the translation, those problems should be his alone. Since the Latin texts varied considerably, his first obstacle was choosing which version to use, and for this he relied extensively on Bible commentaries. Foremost among the commentators was Nicholas of Lyre, a doctor of theology from Paris, who possessed an extraordinary knowledge of Hebrew and of the Talmud. Purvey also consulted what were considered the four principal doctors of the church: Saints Ambrose, Augustine, Jerome, and Gregory.

With several Bibles opened on stands before him, Purvey assigned learned readers to read various passages out loud, line for line, while he sought out explanations in various commentaries. When what he surmised was the correct version—and for this, he also consulted John Wycliffe—a scribe would copy that passage, and the process would begin again.

Unlike Nicholas Hereford, John Purvey resisted the urge to translate word for word based on the various Latin translations. "At the beginning I purposed, with God's help, to make the meaning as true and clear in English as it is in Latin, or more true and more clear than it is in Latin," he wrote.

Finally, when the translation was completed, the Bible needed to be copied by hand, an expensive and time-consuming process that would take ten more years to accomplish. The readers and scribes needed to be paid, and then there were the supplies of ink and vellum to consider. Somehow, there was always enough to continue with the work while John Wycliffe was alive, and even after his death. Many assumed, rightly or wrongly, that John of Gaunt and Joan of Kent provided the necessary financial backing. John of Gaunt was known to be a generous man, and while he could not support John Wycliffe publicly, he could act the part of the loyal patron behind the scenes.

Now that the translation was in good hands, John Wycliffe spent most of his time writing sermons, penning his thoughts about preaching, and working to translate his efforts into English. His primary concern in all preaching was for, as he said, "true biblical exposition." To Wycliffe, the Word of God should be of greatest importance, not the preacher himself. When the preacher was thrust into the foreground, he wrote, "This practice comes from nothing else but the pride of man; everyone seeking his own honor, everyone preaching only himself and not Jesus Christ."

To the end that Scripture should be the focus of all sermons, Wycliffe eschewed worship services that included entertainment or drama of any kind. At the time it was common for minstrels, actors, and acrobats to travel from place to place, offering their services to friars for a meal and a small fee. To Wycliffe, such presentations were only offshoots of the corrupt tastes of the time and should be replaced by the simple presentation of the gospel. Indeed, John Wycliffe wrote vigorously that the preacher should get rid of everything else in the worship service save the reading of the Scripture and a sermon based on God's Word.

When instrumental music began to be added to the

worship service during Wycliffe's lifetime, he wrote of his extreme displeasure. "Christ did not teach His disciples to sing but to preach the gospel," he said. Such performances detracted from devotion to Scripture and, he wrote, "stirred vain men to dancing more than mourning."

At Lutterworth, John adapted a preaching style that would be copied for centuries to come. He divided his sermons into two sections: In the first he explained the meaning of the Scripture for the day, and in the second he expressed the doctrine contained in the Scripture and the moral applications it had for the audience. His rule was never to use an example or give an application that would be beyond the comprehension of the parishioners. Sermons must be plain and simple, and above all, useful—but never boring.

Indeed, John Wycliffe advocated a preaching style that employed evangelistic fervor. "Lift up, wretches, the eyes of your soul and behold Him that no spot of sin was in, what pain He suffered for sin of man!" he cried from the pulpit of St. Mary's. Such fervor was the result of his extreme confidence in Scripture, as demonstrated in another sermon excerpt: "O marvelous power of the Divine Seed! Which overpowers strong men in arms, softens hard hearts, and renews and changes into divine men, men who had been brutalized by sins, and departed infinitely far from God. Obviously such miraculous power could never be worked by the word of a priest, if the Spirit of Life and the Eternal Word did not, above all things else, work with it."

By late 1384, John Wycliffe was considered aged and decrepit, as were most men who were well into their fifties.

The fervor that he had once displayed from the pulpit had lessened considerably, and now he found himself more a participant in the worship service rather than the preacher.

On Holy Innocents Day—December 28, 1384—John was hearing mass at St. Mary's in Lutterworth when he felt a familiar numbness surge through his limbs. As the bread of the Eucharist was lifted high by the priest, the feeble rector collapsed to the floor. When he regained consciousness, he could not move or speak—the paralysis was brought on by his second stroke.

For three days he lingered in this paralyzed state, unable to speak. During that time word spread throughout the country, and to London in particular, that England's most famous heretic lay on his deathbed. Distinguished clerics, including those members of the orders whom Wycliffe had once railed against, rushed to the humble rectory to see the great man's final moments for themselves. John Wycliffe could only open and close his eyes in acknowledgment of their presence. Finally, on December 31, he died. Since he had not been excommunicated—the failure to do so an acknowledgment of his popularity among the people and his friends in high places—his body was buried in consecrated ground at Lutterworth.

Following the burial service, John Purvey redoubled his efforts on completing the Bible translation and the translation of the sermons, working feverishly day and night. When he came across a prayer of John Wycliffe's, he found strength in the words:

Almighty Lord God, most merciful, and in

wisdom boundless, since thou sufferedst Peter and all apostles to have so great fear and cowardice at the time of thy passion, that they flew all away for dread of death, and for a poor woman's voice; and since afterwards, by the comfort of the Holy Ghost, thou madest them so strong that they were afraid of no man, nor of pain, nor death; help now, by gifts of the same Spirit, thy poor servants, who all their life have been cowards, and make them strong, and bold in thy cause, to maintain the gospel against Antichrist, and the tyrants of this world.

Now that John Wycliffe was dead, what would happen to the Lollards, Purvey wondered sadly. Perhaps those who had once boldly spoken out, and then timidly recanted, might now regain their courage. Would fear overcome them, or would they truly "maintain the gospel"?

twelve

The Legacy of Light

After William Courtenay's purging of Oxford, the church turned its attention to other centers of Lollardy in England. With the curious exception of the parish of Lutterworth, Leicestershire became the new focus, and especially the doings of two ringleaders.

William Smith, who was considered the first layman leader, and William Swinderby would be the first two nonacademic leaders of Lollardy. Although their tenure would be short, through their preaching they had touched many lives and, in doing so, secured a future for Lollardy and the teachings of John Wycliffe.

Swinderby, in particular, was a memorable figure. Also known as "William the Hermit" because for a time he lived in the woods, he was excommunicated in 1382 for his preaching. That mandate did not slow him down for long.

From 1382, following the lead of Swinderby, Lollards began meeting in secret, away from heresy-hunting bishops. If there was no public record of Swinderby's or other Lollard activities for a few months or years, that did not mean that Wycliffe's movement was dying out. To the contrary, such pauses more likely indicated that the Lollards had carried their message to more far-flung locales.

When the Lollards found welcome in Hereford, Worcester, and South Wales, they were joined by some old faces. John Aston, a native of Worcester, who had memorably recanted his beliefs at the Convocation of Canterbury, was back within the fold. He first spoke out in September 1383 in Gloucester, where he lambasted the bishop of Norwich's crusade to convert Flemish supporters of Pope Clement of France by force. Afterward, Aston returned to preaching Wycliffe's doctrine as if he had never turned his back.

Joining Aston in late 1385 was none other than Nicholas Hereford, who had been rescued from the Vatican prison by a popular uprising in which the prisons were raided and all prisoners set free. Realizing he was fortunate to leave Italy with his life, Nicholas soon escaped back to England, and in short order began preaching in Worcester. When his presence became the thorn in the side of the local bishop, Nicholas left for Bristol, which was on the border between two dioceses and therefore a relatively safe area.

And at Bristol, the lay preachers and the Oxfordians were joined by John Purvey and a group of artisans who were working to complete the second translation of the

Bible. With Nicholas Hereford assuming leadership of the Lollards, Bristol would be the last stand for the earliest devotees of John Wycliffe. In August 1387, Bishop Henry Wakefield prohibited four men from preaching in the area—Nicholas Hereford, John Aston, John Purvey, and William Swinderby—and one, Nicholas, was arrested. At the same time, the written works the men had distributed were confiscated and burned. One year later, John Aston died.

Rumors abounded of outrageous torture endured by Nicholas while in the custody of William Courtenay. But the tumultuous life of this one-time "brother" of Wycliffe was about to take a few more surprising turns. In December 1391, Nicholas was released from prison and granted the king's protection as he traveled to Herefordshire. There, in what was still a Lollard stronghold, he acted as one of the bishop's assessors in a trial of one of his fellow Lollards. As might be expected, the reaction from the Lollards was swift and furious: Nicholas Hereford was immediately declared a turncoat and became a target for harsh criticism. The criticism escalated when, in February of 1394, Nicholas was promoted to chancellor of Hereford Cathedral and granted such royal favors as a large quantity of meat and wine every year. The saga of Nicholas Hereford ended sometime after 1417 when he gave up all his positions and royal favors and retired to a Carthusian monastery, where he would die an elderly, penniless man.

For William Swinderby, however, there would be no such compromises. When he had been arrested in 1382, he had recanted on some positions, but he nonetheless continued preaching. In 1390, he was denounced again as a heretic, this time in Monmouth, to the far south, indicating how far the movement had indeed spread. In 1391, Swinderby was summoned again, and this time fifteen articles of accusation had been drawn up against him, all of which he vehemently denied. When he was released, he immediately went into hiding and was presumed to have found sanctuary in Wales. Incensed that such a heretic could elude his henchmen, Richard II sent out proclamations for Swinderby's capture, but to no avail.

While the first lay preacher, William Smith, was arrested in 1389 and shortly thereafter admitted the errors of his ways, there would be no clear-cut end of Swinderby's preaching. William Swinderby's contribution to Lollardy was immense and would continue to be felt in the next quarter century. Thanks to his efforts, Wycliffe's teachings would find a warm welcome in a wide area of England, and from a wide swath of society.

In the final decade of the fourteenth century, the new converts to Lollardy were primarily of humble birth and lacking much, if any, formal education. Nonetheless, these advocates were self-taught, serious people, including many devout women who were active but did not hold positions of leadership or patronage. Their attitude became one of not trying to win support of the knights and bishops, as Wycliffe and certain Oxfordians had done, but reforming the church in England.

To that end, in 1395, while the full Parliament was in session, a Lollard bill or manifesto was tacked to the doors of Westminster Hall and St. Paul's Cathedral. The manifesto began as follows:

We poor men, treasurers of Christ and His apostles, denounce to the lords and the commons of the Parliament certain conclusions and truths for the reformation of the holy church of England. . . .

That preamble introduced twelve "conclusions" that the Lollards wanted Parliament to address seriously, among them these matters of contention:

That our usual priesthood which began in Rome, pretended to be of power more lofty than the angels, is not that priesthood which Christ ordained for His apostles. . . .

That the pretended miracle of the sacrament of bread drives all men but a few to idolatry, because they think that the body of Christ which is never away from heaven could by power of the priest's word be enclosed essentially in a little bread which they show the people. . . .

That exorcisms and blessings performed over wine, bread, water, and oil. . .over clothing, mitre, cross, and pilgrim's staves, are the genuine performance of necromancy rather than of sacred theology. . . .

That special prayers for the souls of the dead. . . are a false foundation of alms, and for that reason all houses of alms in England have been wrongly founded. . . .

That auricular confession which is said to be so necessary to the salvation of a man, with its

> *pretended power of absolution, exalts the arro-*
> *gance of priests. . .for both lords and ladies attest*
> *that, for fear of their confessors, they dare not*
> *speak the truth. . . .*

But while Parliament would fail to act on any of the conclusions, the authorities of the church were not so cavalier in their assessment. How could they sit by and do nothing when the common man and woman were being poisoned by preachers in their own "vulgar" tongue? As a first measure, the bishops were given the power in their dioceses to seize any and all Lollard tracts and to punish anyone found owning or distributing such materials. But the ecclesiastical powers wanted total suppression of the heresy inherent in these conclusions. Other European countries burned their heretics at the stake—and yet the harshest penalty England could exact was imprisonment from the government and excommunication from the church. To remedy the situation, the archbishop and bishops first petitioned the king for the death penalty for heretics. Then, to bolster their bold move, William Courtenay wrote to the new pope in Rome, Boniface IX, enclosing the Lollard conclusions for his review. And then they waited.

As expected, an outraged Boniface IX penned his extreme displeasure in a series of letters to Richard II, as well as many officers of the government, all sent in September of 1395. It was his hope that "there may not one spark remain hid under the ashes, but that it be utterly extinguished and speedily put out"—both a figurative and literal comment on the supposed heretics that were thought to be swarming England.

While the Lollards may have felt disheartened at this juncture, they would not remain so for long. Toward the end of 1395, John Purvey completed his second translation of the Bible into English. His newest translation was considered vastly more readable, and Lollard preachers began carrying portions of it wherever they traveled. So much so were these preachers associated with the new Bible that they began to be dubbed "Wycliffe's Bible Men."

Again, the name Wycliffe stirred the already bubbling ecclesiastical cauldron into greater frenzy. In 1396, Thomas Arundel succeeded William Courtenay as archbishop of Canterbury, bringing with him a renewed vigor to attack heresy. In one of his first acts as archbishop, Arundel signed an official order that no one could translate the Bible or use a translation without the approval of his or her bishop or an official of the province. But Arundel, a former bishop and chancellor of England who had known Wycliffe, laid the blame for his order at the grave of the late rector of Lutterworth. "This pestilential and most wretched John Wycliffe of damnable memory," Arundel wrote, "a child of the old devil, and himself a child or pupil of Antichrist, who, while he lived, walking in the vanity of his mind. . .crowned his wickedness by translating the Scriptures into the mother tongue."

Within three years after Arundel was installed, England had a new king, as well. After a series of feuds between the brothers of John of Gaunt and Richard II, the still-young king attempted to confiscate the property of the exiled Henry of Bolingbroke, John of Gaunt's eldest son. When Henry returned to England, he overtook Richard, who then abdicated his throne (and was later murdered), and became king himself. Henry IV, the new king, would reward his supporters generously, and not the least of these would be the archbishop himself.

By 1401, Henry IV had granted the bishops' earlier request, and what would be known as the Statute of Heresy was in place. Under this new law, which allowed heretics to be burned at the stake, there would be two restrictions: The accused must be one who had renounced his false beliefs and then returned to them; and the burning must take place on "a high place."

Now that the power of the government was in his hands, Arundel was eager to enforce the new statute. By February, the deed would be done. England's first martyr, William Sawtrey, was neither an early supporter of John Wycliffe nor an ardent Lollard. First convicted of heresy in 1399 when he was a chaplain, Sawtrey renounced his former beliefs and moved to London where he became parish priest of a small, and he thought insignificant, church. When word of his lapsed preaching reached the receptive ears of the archbishop, Sawtrey was brought in, tried, and executed.

During the same month, one of the most notorious Lollards was also convicted of heresy, but this time the sentence would not lead to death. John Purvey had been more involved with Lollardy than almost anyone, yet amazingly he had never been captured or tried for his beliefs before.

Thus, under the new statute, Purvey was tried and returned to Saltwood Castle prison where his case was personally supervised by William Arundel. One week later, Purvey renounced his "false beliefs" in front of prelates and the primate and was set free. After serving two years as a parish priest in West Hythe, Kent, John Purvey vanished from sight, never to be heard from again.

Despite the monumental loss of the close companion of John Wycliffe, and the ever present threat of the Statute of Heresy, Lollardy was still alive and well. As Wycliffe had once predicted to Purvey, the royal marriage of Richard II to Anne of Bohemia had indeed allowed an exchange of ideas critical to the future of the church. Thanks to the Czech theological students who had accompanied Anne to England, as well as others, Lollardy had now spread across the English Channel, and many miles beyond, to Bohemia.

Among those personally instrumental in this exchange was Jerome of Prague, a scholar and preacher who spent two years at Oxford around the turn of the century. Jerome was able to obtain and carry back to Bohemia almost the entire collection of Wycliffe's written works (which had continued to be copied, despite the best efforts of the church). Within a few years, most of these works had been translated into Czech and copied and were available at centers of higher learning and certain churches, including the University of Prague and Prague's Bethlehem Chapel. A few years later, in 1407, Thomas Ile of Braybrooke gave two visiting Czech students copies of Wycliffe's treatise *On Lordship* to take back with them to Prague. Following their eviction from

Oxford, many Lollards, including John Purvey, had resided for a time in Braybrooke in Northamptonshire.

John Wycliffe's words still had the power to enlighten and inspire—and to turn a new generation toward the possibilities of church reform. In Prague, that generation would be led by Jan Hus, a rector at Bethlehem Chapel, which by the early fourteen hundreds had become a center of the Czech reform movement. Hus had studied at the University of Prague, and he had joined the faculty after graduation as an arts lecturer. His decision to become a priest was motivated more by a desire for prestige and financial security than to win souls for Jesus Christ.

His conversion to Christianity changed the way he thought about everything. Where he had once craved material possessions, he now sought a simpler life, interested solely in spiritual growth. Such an attitude shaped his willingness to accept Wycliffe's ideas, as well as those of earlier Czech theologians. But Hus was more interested in the abuses of the papacy, especially the sale of indulgences and the immorality of priests, than in Wycliffe's position on transubstantiation, which he found to be faulty. By 1407, Jan Hus would be at the forefront of the Czech reform movement, challenging the power the Germans held in the Roman Catholic Church of Bohemia and attacking the papal politics of the Great Schism.

In that same year, William Arundel, exasperated at the ineffectiveness of his office to rid Oxford of heresy, held the Convocation of Canterbury again at Oxford. The dissemination of heretical materials from Oxford had reawakened the archbishop, who now initiated a new policy of censorship. While at Oxford, a committee of twelve appointed by the archbishop reexamined Wycliffe's works to determine which, if any, could be taught in the schools. Despite a brave stand by certain Oxfordians, the primate had his way, and more than 260 heretical or erroneous conclusions were detected in the writings. By mid-1411, by order of the archbishop, Wycliffe's works discovered at Oxford were (again) effectively destroyed.

Those heretical and erroneous conclusions would be one of the subjects discussed some years later at the Council of Constance (1414–1417), held near Lake Constance, Switzerland. In the past, councils would have been called by emperors or popes, but with the Great Schism and the two popes in Rome and Avignon, the Council of Constance was called by a plurality of bishops.

When the bishops examined the writings of John Wycliffe, they concurred with Arundel's earlier assessment. The Council of Constance condemned Wycliffe's writings as heretical on 260 counts—and ordered the long-dead heretic's bones to be exhumed and burned. Then the bishops turned their attention to Jan Hus, whom they had promised safe passage and conduct if he would attend the council.

After leaving Prague in 1412 for southern Bohemia, Hus had continued preaching doctrine contrary to the church. Rather than venerating the pope, Hus preached of a faith centered on Christ, and he stressed an individual's responsibility before God. Obviously influenced by John Wycliffe, Hus believed that only God could forgive sins.

But the day of immunity for heretics had long passed. At

the Council of Constance, Hus was imprisoned soon after arrival and then put on trial for heresy. Even though he refused to admit that the charges against him were true unless proven by Scripture, he was judged guilty by the bishops. On July 6, 1415, Jan Hus was burned at the stake, and his ashes were thrown into the Rhine River. He had died singing "Kyrie eleison," or "Lord, have mercy [upon us]."

Unlike many of Wycliffe's earlier supporters, Hus had not renounced his beliefs. Hus's followers, known as Hussites, would continue to preach the doctrines Jan Hus cherished, much as the Lollards had done for John Wycliffe. A century or so later when the movement had spread to Germany, the theologian Martin Luther would embrace many of Hus's beliefs as the Protestant Reformation was born.

In 1415, Philip Repingdon was the bishop of Lincoln, a diocese that included the parish church of Lutterworth. When he received the order from the Council of Constance to exhume the bones of John Wycliffe, he knew he was being ordered to act right away. Still, days and then months went by, and the former Lollard who had preached so eloquently on Corpus Christi Day years earlier did nothing.

To the bishop, he had no right to visit the lovingly tended cemetery where John Wycliffe's bones lay so peacefully. He had once declared his beloved mentor a heretic; he would not desecrate his memory further. And so, despite the imposing authority of such ecclesiastical power, Philip Repingdon left John Wycliffe's grave undisturbed.

Twelve years later, the order to exhume the bones of

John Wycliffe was once again given. This time Philip Repingdon's successor carried out the order, on December 16, 1427. As directed, the bones were burned until they were nothing more than ashes. The ashes then were thrown into the River Swift that flowed not far from St. Mary's Church.

As a man, John Wycliffe had been small and frail. But as a force for change, clinging with every breath to the words of Scripture, he became for many generations larger than life. No acts of suppression erased his writing; no threats succeeded in vanquishing his ideas. Into a world of dark, repressive dogma and superstition, John Wycliffe became the first ray of light of what would become a monumental spiritual awakening. He was indeed the Herald of the Reformation.

appendix

A Sampling of the Sermons of John Wycliffe

STEADFAST FAITH

The ground of all goodness is steadfast faith, or belief. This, through grace and mercy, is obtained from God. Faith was the principal ground that enabled the woman of Canaan to obtain health of soul and of body from Christ, for her daughter, who was evil treated by a devil, as the Gospel relates. And the centurion was much praised of Christ for the steadfast belief that he had in the power of His Godhead. Faith is likened to the North Star, for it shows the haven of grace to men rowing in the sea of this world. Faith is the eastern star that leads spiritual kings to worship Jesus Christ.

Faith or belief is as a stone lying in the foundation of a

161

strong building that bears up all the work. For as the building stands firmly that is well grounded upon a stone, so each virtuous deed is strong when it is grounded upon the solidity of belief. For upon this stone, that is, solid faith, Christ said that He would build His church, that is, man's soul.

A man that has lost his right eye is unable to defend himself in battle, for his shield hides his left eye, and so he has no sight to defend himself from the enemy; even so he that has lost the right eye of true faith is unable to withstand or fight against his spiritual enemy, the devil. Saints, as St. Paul says, through steadfastness and true faith overcame kingdoms (Hebrews 11).

The lack of steadfast faith is the chief reason why men fall into deadly sin. Christ said to His disciples that if their faith were as great as the seed of mustard, and they should say to this hill, "Move from here," it should move; and nothing should be impossible to them.

While Peter had true faith, he walked upon the sea as upon dry land; but when the firmness of his faith failed, he began to sink, and therefore Christ reproved him for being of little faith. So it is with us, who are staggering and unsteadfast with the wind of each temptation or fear.

Therefore, brethren, let us set all our belief and full trust on Him who is almighty, and not in any vain thing that may fail in any time. We must trust steadfastly that nothing may harm us any more than He will allow it, and all things which He sends come for the best. And let no wealth of this failing world, neither tribulation, draw our hearts from firm belief in God. Let us not put our belief or trust in charms, or in dreams, or any other fantasies; but only in Almighty God.

To believe in God, as St. Augustine says, is in belief to cleave to God through love, and to seek busily to fulfill His will; for no man truly believes in God, except he that loves God. And no man sins against God except when he fails in belief, which is the ground of all good works.

Riding Toward Heaven or Hell

St. Paul says, "Clothe yourselves in the armor of God, that ye may firmly stand against temptations and deceits of the fiend." Man's body is like clothes with which his soul is covered; and as a horse that bears his master through many perils. And from this horse, that is man's body, many things are required if he will bear his master aright out of perils. For no knight can safely fight against his enemy unless his horse be obedient to him; no more can the soul fight against the wiles of the fiend, if the flesh, which is his horse, live in lusts and likings at his own will.

For Holy Scripture says, "He that nourishes his servant," that is, his own body, "delicately or lustfully shall find it rebel when he least expects." As soon as man begins to live wisely, and flees all the lusts and desires and vanities, which he before was used to and loved, and bows himself under the yoke of God's holy doctrine, then his enemies begin to contrive by wiles, frauds, and temptations, to make him fall. And therefore it is needful that his horse be submissive and helping his master to overcome his enemies. For if the soul and the body be well agreed together, and either of them helps the other in this spiritual contest, the fiend shall soon flee and be overcome. For Holy Scripture says, "Withstand ye the fiend, and he shall flee from you."

But it is great folly for any man to fight upon an unbridled horse, and if the horse be wild and ill taught, the bridle must be heavy and the bit sharp to hold him again. And if the horse be easy and obedient to his master, his bridle shall be light and smooth, also.

The bridle is called abstinence, with which the body shall be restrained, that he have not all his own way, for he is wild and willful, and loath to bow to goodness. With this bridle, his master shall restrain him, to be meek and bow to his will. For if he will fight without a bridle upon him, it is impossible for him not to fall.

But this bridle of abstinence should be led by wisdom, so that nature be held by strength, and the wildness of our nature be restrained by this bridle. For otherwise his horse will fail at the greatest need, and harm his master, and make him lose the victory.

This bridle must have two strong reins, by which you direct your horse at your will; also they must be even, and neither pass the other in length. For if you draw one faster than the other, your horse will swerve aside and go out of the way. Therefore, if your horse shall stay in the middle of the way, it is necessary to draw the reins of the bridle even.

The one rein of the bridle is too loose when you allow your flesh to have its will too much, in eating and drinking, in speaking, in sleeping, in idle standing or sitting, and trivial tale-telling, and all other things that the flesh desires beyond measure and reason. The other rein of the bridle is held too tight when you are too stern with your own body and abstain from having what it should reasonably have.

Whoever pulls either of these reins unevenly will make his horse swerve aside and lose the right way. If you allow your body to have its full liking, that which should be your friend becomes your decided foe. If you withhold that which it ought to have to sustain its nature, as its need requires, then you destroy its strength and its might, so that it cannot help you as it should. Therefore sustain your horse that it faint not, nor fail at your need. And withdraw from it that which might turn you to folly.

Yet your horse needs to have a saddle, to sit upon him the more securely and gracefully in other men's sight. This saddle is gentleness or easiness. That is, whatsoever you do, be it done with good consideration, wisely thinking it through from the beginning to the ending, and what may happen as result; and that it be done sweetly and meekly, and with gentleness. That is, that you calmly suffer slanders and scorns, and other harms that men do against you, and neither grieve yourself in word nor in deed. And though your flesh be aggrieved, keep calmness in heart, and let not any wicked words come from your mouth or tongue, and then you shall be made glad.

As the prophet says, "The calm and the submissively suffering shall result in joy forever for those who do gently with easiness and love, whatsoever they do; so that their out-ward and inward semblance and cheer, be so gentle and lovely in word and deed, that others may be turned to good by their example." This virtue, gentleness of heart and of appearance, makes man gracious to God, and attractive to man's sight, as a saddle makes a horse attractive and worthy of praise.

Two spurs are needed for your horse, and they must be sharp to prick the horse that he loiter not in his way, for many horses are slow if they are not spurred. These two spurs are love and dread, which of all things most stir men to the way of heaven.

The right spur is the love that God's dear children have

for the lasting prosperity that shall never end. The left spur is dread of the pains of hell, which are without number, and never may be counted out. With these two spurs prick your horse if he be dull and unwilling to stir himself to good. And if the right spur of love be not sharp enough to make him go forward on his journey, prick him with the left spur of dread to rouse him.

Separate thy soul from thy body by inward thought, and send thy heart before, into that other land [heaven] and do as a man would do, that must choose between two dwelling places into which when he had once entered he must dwell forever. Certainly, if he were wise, he would send before some of his near friends to see what these places were.

Two places are ordained for man to dwell in after this life. While he is here, he may choose, by God's mercy, which he will; but once he has gone from here he may not do so. For whichever he first goes to, whether he like it well or ill, there he must dwell forevermore. He shall never after change his dwelling, though he hates it ever so badly. Heaven and hell are these two places, and in one of them, each man must dwell.

In heaven is more joy than may be told with tongue, or thought with heart; and in hell is more pain than any man may suffer. With these two spurs awake your horse, and send your heart before, as a secret friend, to espy these dwelling places, what they are.

In hell you shall find all that heart may hate, empty of all good, plenty of all evil that may hurt any thing in body or in soul: hot fire burning, darkness, brimstone most

167

offensive, foul storms and tempests, greedy devils open-mouthed as raging lions, hunger and thirst that never shall be quenched, weeping and wailing and gnashing of teeth, and thick darkness. All hate each other as the foul fiend, and constantly curse the time that they wrought sin.

Above all things they desire to die, and they are ever dying, and fully die they never shall, but ever dying live in pain and woe. They hated death while they lived here, but now they would rather have it than all the wide world. They shall think upon no good, and have no knowledge but of their pains, and sins that they have done. And of all these pains, and many more sorrows than we can tell, the end shall never come.

When you understand that the deadly sin which man has done shall be paid for so dearly with that everlasting pain, then you would desire rather to let thy skin be torn from thy flesh, and thy body hewn to pieces, than to willfully commit a deadly sin—this spur of dread shall make our horse awake, and keep him in the right way, and speed him fast forward, and cause him always to flee from deadly sin, which is thus dearly bought, and make man to be thus bitterly pained forever.

And this is the right spur that should quicken your horse to speed in his way, that you learn to love Jesus Christ, in all your living. And therefore send your thoughts into that land of life, where there is no disease of any kind, neither age nor sickness, nor any other grievance. And who goes there shall find a gracious fellowship, the orders of angels and of all holy saints, and the Lord above them, who gladdens them all.

There is plenty of all good, and absence of all things that

may grieve. There are fairness and riches, honor and joy that each man may feel; love and wisdom that shall last forever. There is no disease that men suffer here: not hypocrisy nor flattery nor falsehood, envy, and ire. Banished from there are thieves and tyrants, cruel and greedy men that pillage the poor, proud men and boasters, covetous ones and beguilers, those that are slothful and licentious, all such are banished out of that pure land.

For there is nothing that men may fear, but instead pleasure and joy and mirth at will, melody and song of angels, bright and lasting bliss that never shall cease. And though they were sick and feeble while they lived here, they shall be so strong there, that nothing shall move against their will. They shall have such great freedom that nothing shall be contrary to their liking. The saved bodies shall never have sickness, or anger, or grievance.

Also they shall be filled with joy in all their senses; for as a vessel that is dipped in water or other liquid is wet within and without, above and beneath, and also all about, and no more liquid can be within it, even so shall those that are saved be fulfilled with all joy and bliss. Also they shall have endless life in the sight of the Holy Trinity, and this joy shall pass all other. They shall be in full security that they will never lose that joy, nor be put out thereof. They shall see Him, both God and man, and they shall see themselves in Him also. They shall also have perfect love to each other, for every one shall agree with the other's desire. And these joys and many more than any tongue of man can fully tell, shall those have that shall be saved, both in body and soul, after the day of doom.

This is the right spur, which should stir men joyfully to love Jesus Christ, and to hasten in the heavenly way. For so sweet is the bliss there, and so great withal, that whoever tastes a single drop of it would be so rapt in liking of God, and of heavenly joy, and he would have such a longing to go there, that all the joy of the world would seem pain to him. This love would move such a man to live more virtuously, and to flee from sin, a hundred times more than any dread of the pain of hell. For perfect love puts out all dread, and cleanses the soul from filth, and makes it to see God, and to flee oft to heaven in its desires, hoping to dwell there forever.

THE NAME OF JESUS

Whosoever desires to love God, if you will neither be deceived nor deceive, if you will be saved and not fail, if you will stand and not fall, study to have this name Jesus constantly in mind. If you do this, the enemy shall fall and you shall stand, and the enemy shall be enfeebled and you shall be strengthened. Therefore, seek this name, Jesus, hold it and forget it not. Nothing so quenches flames, restrains evil thoughts, cuts away venomous affections, or alienates from us vain occupations.

This name, Jesus, truly held in mind, roots up vices, plants virtues, brings charity or love to men, gives men a taste of heavenly things, removes discord, produces peace, gives everlasting rest, and does away with fleshly desires. All earthly desires, all earthly things, it turns into heaviness. It fills those that love it with spiritual joy. The righteous man deserves to be blessed, for he hath truly loved this name, Jesus. He is called righteous, because he seeks earnestly to love Jesus. What can go wrong for him who unceasingly yearns to love Jesus? He loves and he desires to love, for thus we know the love of God to stand; for the more we love, the more we yearn to love.

It is said, "They that eat me shall not hunger, and they that drink me, shall not thirst." Therefore the love of Jesus by itself is delectable and desirable. Therefore no joy shall be lacking for those that seek earnestly to love Him whom angels desire to behold. Angels see Him always, and ever desire to see Him; for they are filled so full that their filling does not take away their desire, and they desire so much that their desire does not take away their fullness. This is full joy; this is glorious joy.

Therefore many men wish to joy with Christ, but as they love not His name, Jesus, they shall have sorrow without end, whatever they do. And if they give all things that they have to poor men, unless they love this name, Jesus, they shall labor in vain. For only such shall be gladdened in Jesus who have loved Him in this present life. Those that defame Him with vices and foul thoughts, and turn not again, there is no doubt but they are put out from the glory of God. Therefore a man shall not see the glory of God that has not joyfully loved this name Jesus.

In truth, an evil man does not find Jesus for he sees Him not where he is. He tries to seek Jesus in the joys of this world, where He shall never be found. Why therefore do you say, "We shall be saved in Jesus," while you cease not to hate Him, without whom you cannot have health?

I am not surprised that a man, being tempted, falls, if he does not have the name of Jesus lasting in his mind. Truly this name cleanses the conscience, makes the heart clear and clean, and drives away fear. It gets a man warmth of love and lifts up the mind to heavenly melody.

O what a good name! O what a sweet name! O glorious name! O healthful name! O name to be desired! Wicked spirits will not abide with you when they behold Jesus, either in mind or hear you proclaim His name out loud. I sought to love Jesus, and ever the more I grew complete in His love, so much the sweeter His name became to me. Therefore, blessed be the name of Jesus forever and ever. Amen.

THE LOVE OF JESUS

Unless a man be purified first by trials and sorrows, he may not come to the sweetness of God's love. O everlasting love, inflame my mind to love God, that it burn not except to His callings. O good Jesus! Who else could give to me what I feel from You? You must now be felt and not seen. Enter into the inmost recesses of my soul; come into my heart and fill it with Your most clear sweetness; make my mind to drink deeply of the strong wine of Your sweet love that I, forgetting all evils, and all trivial thoughts, and disbelieving imaginations, may embrace You only, joyfully rejoicing in my Lord Jesus.

Most sweet Lord, from henceforward leave me not, dwell with me in Your sweetness; for only Your presence is to me solace or comfort, and only Your absence leaves me sorrowful. O Holy Ghost, who inspires where You will, come into me, draw me to You, that I may despise and set at nought in my heart all things of this world. Inflame my heart with Your love that shall forever burn upon Your altar. Come, I beseech You, sweet and true joy; come sweetness so to be desired; come, my beloved, who is all my comfort.

There are three degrees of Christ's love. Those who are chosen for God's love go from one to another. The first is called insuperable, the second is inseparable, and the third is called singular.

Love is insuperable when it cannot be overcome with any other affection or love, or trial or temptation—when it gladly casts down all other hindrances, and all temptations, and quenches fleshly desires. When man suffers gladly and submissively all anguish for Christ, and is not overcome with any delight or flattering—so that whether you are in ease or in anguish, in sickness or in health, you would not for all the world, anger God at any time—that is insuperable love. And blessed is the soul that is in this state. Every labor is light to him that loves truly, neither can any man better overcome labor than by love.

Love is inseparable when man's mind is inflamed with great love and cleaves to Christ by inseparable thought. Such a man does not allow Christ to be any moment out of his mind, but as though he were bound in the heart, he thinks upon, and with great earnestness he draws his spirit from God. Therefore, the love of Christ so grows in the heart of the lover of God, and the despiser of the world, that it may not be overcome by any other affection or love. When man clings to Christ continuously, thinking upon Him, forgetting Him for no other occasion, then man's love is said to be inseparable and everlasting. And what love can be more or greater than this?

The third degree of love is singular. If you seek or receive any other comfort than from your God, even though you love highly, you have not loved singularly. This degree is highest and most wonderful to attain, for it has no equal. Singular love is when all warmth and comfort is closed out of the heart, except the love of Jesus alone. Other delights or joys fail to please, for the sweetness of Him is so comforting and lasting, His love is so burning and gladdening, that he who is in this degree may feel with joy the fire of love burning in his soul. That fire is so pleasant that no man can speak of it except he that feels it, and then not fully.

Then the soul is Jesus loving, on Jesus thinking, and Jesus desiring, burning in longing only for Him, singing in Him, resting on Him. Then the thought turns to song and melody. The soul that is in this degree may boldly say, I mourn for love! I languish to come to my loved Jesus.

This degree of love comes because of man's merit, but God gives it freely to whom He knows is able to take it, and only where there is already great grace. Therefore, let no man presume more of himself than God has called him to. But he that most withdraws his love from the world, and from unreasonable lusts, shall be most able, and most speedily increase in these degrees of love. Those that have liking in things other than Jesus, and in the sweetness of His law, come not to this degree of love.

In the first degree are some, in the second but few, and in the third scarcely any. For the higher the living is, and the more it profits, the fewer lovers it has, and the fewer followers.

The apostle Paul says, "Some are like the light of the sun, some like the moon, and some like the stars." And so it is of the lovers of Jesus Christ. He that is in this degree of love desires to be unbound from the bond of his body, and to be in full joy with Jesus, whom he loves. Therefore such a one in mourning for his long wait may sing this song to his beloved Jesus: "When wilt Thou come, my beloved, to comfort me and bring me out of care, and give Thyself to me, that I may see Thee and dwell with Thee for evermore? My beloved, more than any other, when shall my heart break that I sorrow no more? Thy love hath wounded my heart, and I am desirous to depart. I stand still mourning for one lovely to love." His love draws me. The bond of His love holds me away from worthless places and amusements, till I may get Him—the sight of my beloved who never shall go away.

Thus love moves a soul in which it dwells to sing of his beloved, ever having the heart looking upward to the joys above. And this brings out love tears, languishing for joy. But these words are not pleasant to a fleshly soul. Love is a burning desire to God, with a wonderful delight in soul. Love unites the lover and the beloved. Love is the desire of the heart, ever thinking on that which it loves. Love is a stirring of the soul to love God for Himself, and all other things for God. This love puts out all other love that is against God's will. Love is a right will, turned from all earthly things, and joined to God without departing, accompanied with the fire of the Holy Ghost.

Therefore take on love as the iron takes on the redness of fire, as air does in the sun, as the wool in the dye. The coal heats the iron in the fire so that it is all fire; the air is infused by the sun so that it is all light; and wool takes the hue so that it changes all to the color.

In this manner shall a lover of Jesus Christ be. He shall so burn in love that he shall be wholly turned into the fire of love; he shall so shine in virtues that no part of him be dark in vices.

OF MEEKNESS

No soul can attain to any degree of true love to Jesus unless he is truly meek. For a proud soul seeks to have his own will, and so shall he never come to any degree of God's love. The lower that a soul sits in the valley of meekness, the more streams of grace and love come to him. And if the soul be high in the hills of pride, the wind of the fiend blows away from him all manner of goodness. Therefore as St. Augustine bids, "Whoever wishes to attain to the bliss that is in heaven above, let him set the ground of his foundation here low in meekness." Nothing more overcomes the fiend than meekness, and therefore he hates it so much.

By two things principally may a man know whether he is meek. If his heart be not moved, though his own will be contradicted and criticized—and when he is despised, falsely accused, and slandered; if his will stands unmoved, not desiring revenge, and his mouth be shut from answers that are not meek. For he that has entered truly into God's love is not grieved, whatsoever slander, shame, or reproof he suffers for the love of his Lord. He is glad that he is worthy to suffer pain for Christ's love.

Thus, Christ's disciples went in joy from the council of the Jews, that they were worthy to suffer wrongs for the name of Jesus. For the apostle said, "All that will live meekly, and please Jesus Christ, shall suffer persecutions, and by many tribulations we must enter into the Kingdom of God. For it is given to such, not only that they believe in Christ, but also that they suffer for him." The prophet of God affirms, "Those that sought to do me evil spake vanities and thought deceit all day; but I as deaf heard not, and was as a dumb man not opening his mouth."

By seven tokens a man may suppose that he has the love of Christ.

The first is when all coveting of earthly things, and fleshly lusts, is weakened by Him. For where coveting is, there is not the love of Christ. If a man does not covet, it is a sign that he has love.

The second is a burning desire for heaven. For when he has felt anything of heaven, the more he feels the more he wants, and he that has felt nothing, desires nothing.

The third token is if his tongue has changed. That which used to speak of earth now speaks of heaven.

The fourth is exercise or practicing what is for spiritual good—as when a man, leaving all other things, has good will and devotion to prayer, and finds sweetness therein.

The fifth is when things which are hard in themselves are made easy through love.

The sixth is hardiness of soul to suffer all anguishes and troubles that befall. All the other tokens are not sufficient without this, for he that is righteous hates nothing but sin. He loves God alone; he has no joy but in God; he fears nothing except to offend God. And all his hope is to come from God.

The seventh is joyfulness of soul when he is in tribulation, and that he love God, and thank Him in all diseases that he suffers. It is the greatest token that he has the love of God: No woe, tribulation, or persecution can bring him down from this love. Many love God, as they think, while they are in ease, but in adversity, or in sickness, they hold grudges against God, thinking that they do not deserve so to be punished for any sin they have done. And oft times some say that God does them wrong. All such are feigned lovers, and have not the true love of God. For the Holy Ghost says, "He that is a true friend loveth at all times."

Three principal advantages come from meekly suffering sickness. It cleanses the soul from sin done before; it keeps it from those into which it was likely to fall; it increases the reward in heaven, and gilds the crown; and the longer it endures, the brighter becomes the crown. And in trust hereof St. Paul said that he would joy gladly in his sickness, that the power of Christ dwell in him.

TURNING TO GOD

Christ, not compelling, but freely counseling each man to a perfect life, says thus: "If any man will come after me let him deny himself and take his cross and follow me." Then let us forsake ourselves, that is, what we have made ourselves by sinning, and dwell as those who are changed by grace.

If a proud man be converted to Christ, and is made meek, he has forsaken himself. If a covetous man ceases to covet, and gives away his own things, he has denied himself. If an evil liver changes his life, he has denied himself. The cross of Christ is taken up when compassion and pity toward our neighbor are truly kept, when man is crucified to the world, and the world crucified to him, setting the joy thereof at nothing.

But let us not be so sure of the Lord's mercy that we heap sins upon sins, neither say we while we are young, "Let us follow our desires, and in the end when old, repent from our sins, for the Lord is merciful, He shall not remember our sins." Lord Jesus, turn us to You, and then we shall be turned. Heal us, and we shall be truly whole. For without Your grace and help no man may be truly turned or healed. For they are but scorners who today turn to God, and tomorrow turn away.

What is turning to God? Nothing but turning from the world, from sin, and from the fiend. What is turning from God? Nothing but turning to the changeable goods of the world, to pleasing likeness of creatures, to works of the fiend, and to lusts of the flesh. To be turned from the world is to set at nothing, and to put out of mind all likings, joys, and mirths thereof, and to suffer meekly all bitterness, slanders, and troubles thereof, for the love of Christ; and to leave all occupations unlawful and unprofitable to the soul so that man's will and thought be dead as far as seeking any thing of the world.

Therefore the prophet speaks in the person of souls perfectly turning to God, saying, "Mine eyes," that is, my thought and intent, "shall ever be to God. For he shall draw my feet," that is, my soul and my affections, "out of the snare, and the net of love of this world." He that is truly turned to God flees from vices and beholds not the solaces or comforts of this world. He sets his mind so steadfastly on God that he well might forget all outward things; he gathers himself all within; he is lifted up wholly into Christ.

Those that will turn truly to Christ must flee occasions, words, sights, and deeds that tempt them to sin. For when the fiend sees one among a hundred who withstands his enticings and turns to God, following the steps of Christ, despising the joys of this present life, and seeking to love everlasting heavenly things, he finds a thousand deceits to ensnare and trouble him, and a thousand manner of temptations to cast him down from God's love to the love of the world. And he begins with the smallest, that by foul thoughts he may make him to be foul toward God.

He brings to man's mind the lusts which he had before, and suggests to him that he does not need to leave all his worldly and fleshly likings. The fiend says, "It is too hard for a man to depart from all pleasure." He stirs up fantasies, vain thoughts innumerable, and unprofitable affections which before were asleep.

The fiend rears against such a soul; he slanders, and is guilty of backbiting, persecutions, tribulations, false challenges, false accusations of various sins, and all manner of hatred. He calls again to mind the delight man had in things he loved before. He enflames the heart and the flesh with foul burnings. He begins by small enticings, and pursues to the greatest flame of wickedness. And he works thus busily to blow against us all manner of temptations and tribulations, because he sees that by the mercy of God we are escaped out of his power. For he seeks nothing so much as to separate a man from the holy and everlasting love of Jesus Christ, and to make him love failing things and the uncleanness of this world.

To Be Tempted

He that is truly fed with the bread that came down from heaven bows not his love to those things to which the fiend entices. Temptations are overcome by patience and meek suffering. What is patience? A glad and willing suffering of troubles. He that is patient murmurs not at adversity, but rather, at all times, praises God.

Evil men always grudge in adversities, and flee from them as much as they may. For as long as they are totally given to material things, they are deprived of true hope of everlasting things. They find solace or comfort only in earthly goods, for they have lost the taste for heavenly things.

There is no soul of man in this world that clings not either to the Creator or the things created. If he loves the created he loses God, and goes to death with that which he loves. Such love in the beginning is hard labor and folly, in the middle it is languor and wretchedness, and in the end it is hate and pain.

He that truly loves his maker refuses to desire any things that are in the world. It is sweetness for him to speak of Him and be with Him; to think upon his maker is refreshing to him. He closes his outer senses lest death enter in by the windows, lest he be occupied unprofitably with any vanity. Sometimes there are reared against him reproofs, scorns, and slanders. Therefore it is needful that he take the shield of patience, and be ready to forget and to forgive all wrongs, and to pray for the turning to good of them that hate him and hurt him.

No man knows his true self, whether he be strong or feeble, unless he is tempted when he is at peace. Many men seem to be patient when they are not in trouble, but when a light blast, not of injustice but of correction, touches them, their mind quickly turns into bitterness and wrath, and if they hear one word said against their will, they reply with two stronger ones. Into their counsel come not, O my soul!

The darts of the enemy are to be quenched with the meekness and sweetness of the love of Christ. Do not give way to temptation, be it ever so grievous. For the greater the battle, the more glorious the victory, and the higher the crown. Blessed is the man that suffers temptation, for when he is proved to be true, he shall take a crown of life. Flee as much as you can from the praising of men. Despise favor, worship, and all vain glory, and gladly sustain or suffer enmities, hates, backbiting, and reproofs. And so by a bad name, and by good praise, by tribulations and gladness, cease thou not to press forward to heavenly kingdoms.

When thou art tempted or troubled, think upon the remedy that our Savior says in His Gospel: "Watch ye and pray ye, that ye enter not into temptation." He does not say, "Pray ye that ye be not tempted." For it is good and profitable for good men to be tempted and troubled, as is shown by what the prophet says: "To him that is tempted and troubled, God saith, I am with him in tribulation; I shall deliver him, and shall glorify him."

Let no man think himself to be holy because he is not tempted, for the holiest and highest in life have the most temptations. The higher a hill is, the greater is the wind at the top; so it follows that the higher the life is, the stronger is the temptation of the enemy.

God plays with His child when He allows him to be tempted, as a mother rises from her much beloved child and hides herself, and leaves him alone and allows him to cry, "Mother, Mother," so that he looks about, cries and weeps for a time, and at last when the child is ready to be overset with troubles and weeping, she comes again, clasps him in her arms, and kisses him, and wipes away the tears. So our Lord allows His beloved child to be tempted and troubled for a time, and withdraws some of His solace and full protection, to see what His child will do; and when he is about to be overcome by temptations, then He defends him, and comforts him with His grace. And therefore, when we are tempted, let us cry for the help of our Father, as a child cries after the comfort of its mother. For whoso prays devoutly, shall have help oft to pray. Devout prayer of a holy soul is as sweet incense that drives away all evil savors, and enters up as an odor of sweetness into the presence of God.

OUR HEAVENLY CHARTER

Every wise man that claims his heritage, asks great pardon, keeps busy, and oft has his mind upon the charter of that which he claims. Therefore, let each man learn to live virtuously, and keep his mind upon the charter of heaven's bliss, and study steadfastly the meaning of this decree, for the pardon thereof shall endure without end.

Understand well that the charter of this heritage, and the infallible decree of this everlasting pardon, is our Lord Jesus Christ, written with all the might and goodness of God.

The parchment of this heavenly charter is neither of sheepskin nor of calf, but it is of the body of our Lord Jesus, a lamb that never was spotted with spot of sin. And there never was skin of sheep or of calf so sorely and so hard strained upon the tools of any parchment maker as the blessed body of our Lord Jesus Christ, which for our love was strained and drawn upon the cross.

No man ever heard from the beginning of the world until now, nor shall hear from hence to doomsday, that a writer ever wrote upon sheepskin or upon calfskin with such hard and hideous pens, so bitterly, so sorely, and so deeply as the accursed Jews wrote upon the blessed body of our Lord Jesus Christ, with hard nails, sharp spear, and sore pricking thorns instead of their pens. They wrote so sorely and so deep that they pierced His hands and feet with hard nails. They opened His heart with a sharp spear. They pressed upon His head a crown of sharp thorns. The wounds upon that blessed body are the letters with which our charter was written, by which we may claim our heritage, if we live rightly, and keep the charter steadfastly in mind.

The subject of the words written within and without this blessed charter, and body of Jesus Christ, is our belief. For He is the strongbox in whom is enclosed and locked all this treasure of knowledge and wisdom of God.

Upon this blessed charter was written wailing, or mourning, and sorrow. Wailing or mourning for sorrow of our sins—which in order to be healed and washed away, Christ, God and man, must suffer such hard and painful wounds. Upon Christ's body, that is, our heavenly charter, was written joy and singing, to all those that completely forsake their sins. For they have full medicine and help, by virtue of the bitter wounds and precious blood of Jesus. And upon the wounds of Jesus may be read sorrow for all them that for wrong desire and lust which endures but a while, bind themselves to sin and serving the fiend, and lose the help of the heavenly charter, and so lose their heritage, and go blindly to sorrow that endures forever.

The laces of this heavenly charter are the promises of God, and those of a God who may not lie, for He is sovereign truth.

The first is His promise that whatever day or hour a sinful man or woman leave their sin, wholly and heartily, with bitter sorrow and turn to Him, He shall receive them in His mercy. But let each man beware that he tarries not too long, lest for his carelessness grace be taken from him.

The second is the full trust we have that God may not lie, neither be false in His promise. And herein depends surely our trust of our heritage. By these two hang the seal of our charter, sealed with the blood of the Lamb, even Christ.

The print of this seal is the form of our Lord Jesus hanging for our sin on the cross. He has His head bowed down, ready to kiss all those that truly turn to Him. He has His arms spread abroad, ready to embrace them. He is nailed fast, hand and foot, to the cross, for He will dwell with them, and never go away from man, but man forsook Him first through sin. He has all His body spread out to give Himself wholly to us, and He has His side opened, and His heart cloven for our sake, so that without hindrance we may creep into Christ's heart, and rest there by steadfast belief and hearty love.

This charter no fire can burn, nor water drown, nor thief rob, nor any creature destroy. For this Scripture the Father of heaven hath made secure, and sent it into the world, Scripture which may not be undone, as the Gospel witnesses. This Scripture is our Lord Jesus Christ, the charter of our heritage of heaven.

Lock not this charter in thy strongbox but put it, or write it in your heart, and none of the creatures, either in heaven or on earth or in hell, can steal it or tear it from you; but if you govern thyself from assenting to sin, and keep well this charter in the strongbox of your heart with good living and devout love, all thy days—as surely and truly as He is the true God, by virtue of this charter, you shall have your heritage of bliss, enduring without end.

Therefore, may we hasten to repentance, as Augustine bids, and let the last day be often before our eyes. Refrain we our bodies from vices and evil coveting, and ever let our hearts think heavenly things, that when we shall arrive there we may fully use heavenly goods. But why? We believe that when our soul shall be unraveled from the bond of flesh, if we have lived well and rightly before God, the companies of angels shall bring us to worship the true Doomsman [Judge].

If we live, as I said, and do those things that are pleasing to God, then peace shall be our compass and security. Then we shall not dread the fiery darts of the devil, nor any manner of enemy that desires to hurt our souls. The flesh shall no more be adversary to the spirit, nor shall we dread any perils. Then the Holy Ghost shall give to us a dwelling in heavenly things, and we, glad and joyful, shall await the day of doom to come, in which the souls of all men shall receive reward for their deeds. Then sinners and men lacking in pity shall perish. And when all these shall deserve to be sentenced to the fire of hell for their sins and their great trespasses, so then, if we have pleased God while we were here in body, we shall have everlasting reward with saints.

Therefore let us despise all things that are vain and failing, that we may receive great glory from Christ. Therefore turn we away from vices and go we to virtues, nor let superfluous words come out of our mouths, for we shall give account for idle words in the day of doom.

Therefore, enjoy the fellowship of godly men, and turn not away your ears from their words. For the words of men that fear God are words of life and holiness of soul to them that hear and understand them. As the sun rising drives away the mist, so the teaching of holy men casts away the darkness from our hearts.

I beseech you, shun proud men, envious men, back-biters, liars, swearers, and men despising their salvation, who are dead to virtues, and joy in their own lusts, and lack God's joy. I speak not only of those that are in your house but wherever you shall hear such, shun them and do not come with such men if you cannot dissuade them from their error. For by one sickly sheep all the flock is defiled, and a little portion of gall turns much sweetness into bitterness. For though a man seem clean in clothing, and noble in bringing forth sweet words, nevertheless if he does the contrary works, his hypocrisy hurts more than his figure or his words can please.

And every work that you think to do, first think about God, and examine diligently whether the work is of God; and if it be rightful before God, perform it, or else cut it away from your soul. And likewise be aware of each wickedness and sin, in word and deed, in thought, in hands, in feet, in sight, and in hearing, and keep we our body and soul.

For Jesus Christ our Lord God, the Son of God the Father, that came down from heaven to earth, He was lifted up on the cross, and died for us sinners, to deliver us from the tormenting of the devil. He suffered pain to deliver us from everlasting pain. He suffered death to deliver us from death. He rose again from death, that we should rise again in body and soul in the last day of the great doom. And therefore it is said of the first church, that one heart, one will, and one soul was in them for the Lord.

Lord, give me grace to hold righteousness in all things; spiritual hardiness and temperance, that I may lead a clean and blessed life, and prudently flee evil, and that I may understand the treacherous and deceitful falseness of the devil, lest he beguile me under the pretense of goodness. Make me mild, willing, peaceable, courteous, and temperate, and to accord goodness without feigning, unto all. And make me steadfast and strong.

And also, Lord, give me the ability to act in mildness, that I be quiet in words, that I speak what is appropriate, and that I speak not that which it is not right to speak. Give me grace to keep the faith unspotted without errors, and that my works henceforth be worthy.

HOW TO PRAY

Our Lord Jesus Christ taught us to pray continually for all needful things, both for our body and our soul. In the Gospel of St. Luke, Christ says it is needful to pray continually, and St. Paul bids Christian men pray without ceasing or hindrance. St. James says that the fervent and lasting prayer of a just man is of much worth.

And while Moses was in the mount, and held up his hands, and prayed for his people, his people had victory over their enemies; and when he ceased to pray thus, his people were overcome, as the second book of Holy Writ teaches. So if priests dwell in the mount of high spiritual life, and espy deceits of the devil, and show them to the people by true preaching, and hold up their hands, that is, open good works, and continue in them; and pray with fervent desire to perform righteousness of God's law and command—then Christian people shall have victory over the devil and cursed sin, and then shall rest and peace and love dwell among them. And if priests cease this holy life and good example, and this desire of righteousness, then Christian people shall be much overcome by sin, and have pestilence and wars, and woe enough; and unless God help, more endless woe in hell.

King Hezekiah, by holy prayer and weeping and sorrow, got forgiveness for his sin, and fifteen years of his life; and the sun went back ten degrees on the dial, as Isaiah's book witnesses. Also by the prayer of the holy leader Joshua, the sun and moon stood still all day, to give light to pursue God's enemies who desired to quench God's name,

His law, and His people.

Therefore Christ says to His disciples, "If ye ask my Father any thing in my name, he shall give it to you"; but we ask in the name of Jesus, when we ask any thing needful or profitable for the saving of men's souls, so we should ask this devoutly, with great desire, and wisely, humbly, and perseveringly by firm faith, true hope, and lasting love; and whatever we ask thus, we shall have of the Father in heaven.

Also Christ says thus in the Gospel, "If ye give good things to your children, how much more shall your Father of heaven give a good Spirit to men that ask him." Then, since nature teaches sinful men to give goods to their children, how much more will God, author of goodness and love, give spiritual goods, profitable to the soul, to His children whom He loves so much! Therefore ask of God heavenly things, such as grace, will, wisdom, and power to serve God, to please Him; and not for worldly goods, except as much as is needful to sustain thy life in truth and service of thy God.

See now how wicked men's prayers displease God, and harm themselves and the people. God Himself speaks in this way to evil men that pray to Him in need: "I have called, and ye have forsaken and have despised all my blamings, and I shall despise your perishing, and shall scorn you. When that which ye have dreaded shall come to you, then ye shall call and I shall not hear, for they hated discipline. They retained not the fear of the Lord, and they assented not to my counsel."

And by the prophet Isaiah, God says thus to wicked men: "Ye princes of Sodom, hear the Lord's word: people of Gomorrah, understand with thine ears the law of our Lord God. Your incense is abomination to me. I shall not suffer your new moon, which is a principal feast and Sabbath, and other feasts. Your companies are evil, my soul hath hated your feasts of months, and solemnities. They are made to me heavy and troublous, and when ye shall hold forth your hands I will turn mine eyes away from you. And when ye shall make many prayers, I will not hear, for your hands are full of blood."

What a wonder it is that men praise God so much by this new praying: by great crying and high song, and leave the still manner of praying as Christ and His apostles did. It seems that we seek our own pleasure and pride in the song, more than the devotion and understanding of what we sing. This is great sin, for Augustine says, "As oft as the song delights me more than that which is sung, so oft I acknowledge that I trespass grievously."

Shall this new song excuse us from learning and preaching the gospel that Christ taught and commanded? Therefore, ye that are priests live well, pray devoutly, and teach the gospel truly and freely, as Christ and His apostles did. Amen.

TWELVE HINDRANCES TO PRAYER

Here follow twelve hindrances to prayer, whereby men may know better why they are not always heard when they pray to God.

The first hindrance to prayer is the sin of him that prays. In Isaiah 59: "Your wickednesses have separated you from your God; and your sins have hidden his face from you, so that he will not hear." And in Jeremiah 5: "Our sins have kept God from us." And in Lamentations 3: "We have done wickedly, and have deserved vengeance; therefore thou mayest not be prayed. And oft thou hast covered thyself with a cloud, that a prayer pass not through." And David says in the Psalter, "If I beheld wickedness in my heart, God shall not hear."

The second hindrance is the doubt of him that prays. In James 1 it is said: "Let a man ask in faith, nothing doubting, for he that doubteth is like a wave of the sea, which is driven of the wind, and tossed about. Let not that man guess that he shall get any thing of the Lord." And Bernard says, "He is proved unworthy to have heavenly blessings, that asketh of God with doubting desire."

The third hindrance is this, that a man asks not that which ought to be asked. In Matthew 20 it is said: "Ye know not what ye ask." Oft the church is not heard, when it ask that tribulations be taken away.

The fourth hindrance is being unworthy of Him to whom we pray. For God in Jeremiah 7 and 11 says, "Pray not thou for this people, for I shall not hear thee." And in Jeremiah 15 God says, "Though Moses and Samuel stand before me, my will is not to this people; cast them out from my face and go they out."

The fifth hindrance is the multitude of evil thoughts. In Genesis 15 Abraham drove away the birds; likewise, he that prays shall drive away evil thoughts.

The sixth hindrance is the despising of God's law. In Proverbs 28 God says, "The prayer of him that turneth away his ear, that he hear not the law of God, shall be abominable, or cursed." And in Proverbs 1, "They shall call me to help [says God], and I shall not hear them; for they hated teaching and chastising."

The seventh hindrance is hardness of soul, and this is of two types. Some hardness is against poor men, of which it is said in Proverbs 21: "If a man stoppeth his ear at the cry of a poor man, he shall cry and he shall not be heard." Another hardness is to them that have trespassed, when a man will not forgive them. In Mark 11, Christ says, "When ye stand to pray, forgive ye, if ye have any thing against any man; that also your Father which is in heaven, forgive you your sins. That if ye forgive not men, neither shall your Father forgive you your sins."

The eighth hindrance is increase of sin. In James 4, He says, "Draw nigh to God, and he shall draw nigh to you." He that draws nigh to God ceases from doing evil work. Concerning this hindrance, and that which goes before, Isidore says, "In two manners a prayer is hindered, that a man may not get the things that are asked; one is if a man do yet evils, that is, willfully continueth in sin; and the other is if he forgive not sin to man that trespasseth against him."

The ninth hindrance is littleness of desire. Augustine

says, "God keepeth that thing from thee, which he will not give soon to thee, that thou learn to desire great things."

The eleventh hindrance is the impatience of him that asks. In 1 Samuel 28, Saul asked counsel of the Lord, and He answered not Saul. And Saul said: "Seek ye for me a woman that hath an evil spirit."

The twelfth hindrance is the lack of perseverance in prayer. In Luke 11, Christ says, "If a man continueth knocking at the gate, the friend [that is, God] shall rise and give him as many loaves as he needeth."

Now you have twelve hindrances to prayer, well grounded in Holy Scripture. It is good, before you pray, to search your conscience, so that your prayer is not hindered by any of these, and so by grace to have the answer to your prayer, and eventually to come to bless without end.

HOW TO LIVE LIFE

First, when you rise, or fully awake, think upon the goodness of your God: how because of His own goodness, and not for any need, He made all things out of nothing, both angels and men, and all other creatures.

Your second thought should be on the great suffering and willing death that Christ endured for mankind. When no man might make payment for the guilt of Adam and Eve, and many others, neither could any angel make payment, then Christ from His endless love, suffered such great passion and painful death, that no creature could suffer so much.

Think thirdly how God has saved you from death and other mischief, and suffered many thousands to be lost the previous night, some in water, and some in fire, and some by sudden death—and some to be damned without end. And for this goodness and mercy thank God with all your heart. And pray that He will give you grace to spend in that day, and evermore, all the powers of thy soul, thy mind, understanding, reason, and will, as well as all the powers of your body, your strength, beauty, and five senses, in His service and worship. Pray too that He will empower you to do nothing against His commandments; but in willing performance of His works of mercy, and in giving a good example of holy life, both in word and deed to all men about you.

Next, be sure that you are well occupied, with no idle time, because of the danger of temptation. Take meat and drink in moderation, not too costly, and be not too particular about them. But such as God sends you with health, take it in such amounts that you will be fresh in mind and understanding to serve God. And always thank Him for such gifts.

Besides this, be sure that you do right and fairly to all men, thy superiors, equals, and subjects or servants, and stir them all to love truth, and mercy, and true peace, and love.

Also, most of all fear God and His wrath, love God and His law, and His worship; and ask not principally for worldly reward. In your heart desire the bliss of heaven, in the mercy of God, and a holy life; and think much of the dreadful doom of pains of hell, in order to keep you from sin.

At the end of the day think where you have offended God, and how much and how often, and therefore be sorrowful, and amend your actions while you may. And think how many God has allowed to perish that day, in many ways, and to be damned everlastingly, and how graciously He has saved you, not for thy deserving, but for His own mercy and goodness, and therefore thank Him with all your heart. And pray to Him for grace that you may dwell and end in His true and holy service and real love, and teach other men to do the same.

If you are a priest and especially one having the charge of souls, live a holy life, surpassing other men in holy prayer, desire, and thinking, in holy speaking, counseling, and true teaching.

And may God's commands, His gospel, and virtues, be ever in your mouth. Despise sin, and seek to draw me from it, and may your deeds be so rightful that no man shall blame them with reason, but may your open deeds be a true book to all your people and unlearned men, to serve God and do His commands thereby. For an example of a good life, one that is open and lasting, stirs men more than true preaching by word only.

And waste not your goods in great feasts of rich men, but live a humble life, of poor men's alms and goods, both in meat and drink and clothes. The remainder give truly to poor men that have not of their own, and may not labor for feebleness or sickness, and thus, you shall be a true priest both to God and man.

If you are a lord, ensure that you live a rightful life in your own person, both in respect to God and man, keeping the commands of God, doing the works of mercy, ruling well your five senses, and doing reason, and equity, and good conscience to all men.

In the second place, govern well your wife, children, and household attendants, in God's law, and allow no sin among them, neither in word nor in deed, that they may be examples of holiness and righteousness to all others. For you shall be condemned for their evil life and their evil example unless you amend those as much as you are able.

In the third place, govern well your tenants, and maintain them in right and reason, and be merciful to them in their rents. And chastise in good manner they that are rebels against God's commands and virtuous life, more than for rebellion against your own cause. Otherwise you love your own cause more than God's, and yourself more than God Almighty, and you will then be a traitor to God. Love, reward, praise, and cherish the true and virtuous of life more than if you sought only your own profit.

And reverence and maintain truly, according to your

skill and might, God's law and true preachers of it, and God's servants, in rest and peace. You do wrong against God if you maintain the Antichrist's disciples in their errors against Christ's life and His teaching, and help to slander and pursue true men that teach Christ's gospel and His life.

If you are a laborer, live in meekness, and truly and willingly do your labor, that your lord or master, if he be a heathen man, by your meekness, willing and true service, may not have a grudge against you, nor slander your God, nor your Christian profession, but rather be stirred to come to Christianity.

And serve not Christian lords with grudging, not only in their presence, but truly and willingly, and in absence. Not only for worldly dread, or worldly reward, but for dread of God and conscience, and for reward in heaven. For God, who has put you in such service, knows what state is best for you, and will reward you more than all earthly lords may, if you truly and willingly obey Him.

And in all things beware of grudging against God and the trials sent by Him, in great labor, long or great sickness, and other adversities. And beware of wrath, of cursing, of speaking evil of man or beast, keeping patience, meekness, and love, both to God and man.

Thus, each man in the three states ought to live, to save himself, and to help others. And thus should good life, rest, peace, and love be among Christian men, and they be saved, and heathen men soon converted, and God magnified greatly.

SUGGESTED FURTHER READING

Fountain, David. *John Wycliffe: The Dawn of the Reformation.*
Southampton: Mayflower Christian Books, 1984.

Hall, Louis Brewer. *The Perilous Vision of John Wycliff.* Chicago:
Nelson-Hall, 1942.

Trevelyan, George Macaulay. *English Social History: A Survey of
Six Centuries.* New York: McKay, 1942.

Zieger, Philip. *The Black Death.* New York: Harper & Row, 1969.

HEROES OF THE FAITH

This exciting biographical series explores the lives of famous Christian men and women throughout the ages. These trade paper books will inspire and encourage you to follow the example of these "Heroes of the Faith" who made Christ the center of their existence. 208 pages each. Only $3.97 each!

Available wherever books are sold.

Or order from:
Barbour Publishing, Inc.
P.O. Box 719
Uhrichsville, Ohio 44683
http://www.barbourbooks.com

If you order by mail, add $2.00 to your order for shipping.
Prices subject to change without notice.